ENVIRONMENTAL EDUCATION AND TRAINING

Environmental Education and Training

Edited by
PATRICIA D PARK
DEBORAH A BLACKMAN
GIN CHONG

Ashgate

Aldershot • Brookfield USA • Singapore • Sydney

Published by
Ashgate Publishing Limited
Gower House
Croft Road
Aldershot
Hants GU11 3HR
England

Ashgate Publishing Company
Old Post Road
Brookfield
Vermont 05036
USA

British Library Cataloguing in Publication Data

Environmental education and training
   1. Environmental education
   I. Park, Patricia D. II. Blackman, Deborah A. III. Chong, Gin
   333.7'07

Library of Congress Catalog Card Number: 97-73877

ISBN 1 85972 443 4

Printed and bound by Athenaeum Press, Ltd.,
Gateshead, Tyne & Wear.

CONTENTS

Preface   vi
Jeremy Cooper

Part I - Introduction
Environmental Education and Training: an Introductory Essay   1
Patricia D Park and Gin Chong

1   Environmental Legal Education - For Whom?   11
    D J Hughes

2   The Essence of an Environmental Law Education   17
    William Howarth

3   Reducing the Impact of Agriculture on Water Quality: Legal Controls or Education? 27
    John Steel

4   Implementation of the Environmental Impact Assessment Process in Sri Lanka -   39
    The Story of the Defeat of a Hydroelectric Dam Project
    William W Westerfield, III and Hemantha Withanage

Part II - Introduction
Financial and Managerial Education   63
Deborah A Blackman and Gin Chong

5   What Should We Bring Into Environmental Education?   65
    Zhichang Zhu

6   Environmental Education: Needs and Implications in Financial Training   74
    Paul Jarvis

7   Environmental Education: Where Does it Fit in Decision-Making?   82
    Deborah A Blackman and Tara G Fleming

8   The Impact of Teaching Ethics and Environmental Accounting   93
    Lynda C Helps

9   Why and How Organisations Provide Employees with Environmental Education   101
    Tara G Fleming and Deborah A Blackman

10 Learning to Choose a "Greener" Route for Small Organisations   114
    Jason Palmer and Rita van der Vorst

Index   122

PREFACE

Jeremy Cooper
Head of Law Faculty, Southampton Institute

It gives me great pleasure to write a Preface to this important collection of essays on the role of education and training in furthering mankind's struggle to defend and protect the natural environment, as we glide into a new millennium. In putting together this collection, the editors, all of whom are senior academics in Southampton Institute's Business School and Law Faculty were clearly mindful of the need to promote the pivotal role of interdisciplinary collaboration in raising the public consciousness of the multi-faceted nature of the environment, and the multiple entry points into the debate upon the best methods to develop and protect it. Science, engineering, economics, business management, accountancy and law can all play a crucial part in this struggle, but none of these disciplines is likely to make headway without a close collaboration with the others. And the clay through which the larger project *environmentalism* is moulded, is education.

The contributors to this volume come from a wide diversity of background disciplines, but they are all linked by their involvement in education. In their essays, they demonstrate how education on environmental protection can take place in a wide variety of settings, ranging from secondary school, to the university law school, to the accountant's office, to the farming estate. They demonstrate that teaching environmentalism is challenging, but exciting, as it demands a lateral approach to subject based teaching, and it demands both courage and imagination. They also make a compelling case for the further penetration by environmentalists of the educational system, which is currently stimulated by an intense interest in the effects of globalisation, emerging at every level of international business and marketing strategy, as free trade couples with a hugely liberalised capital transfer facility, fuelled by a technological communications explosion, to change the face of the globe. Furthermore, they demonstrate the immense opportunity afforded to the world's environmentalist community to reach out to the idealism that lies too often untapped in the hearts of so many of the new generation of young people who find themselves fearful of the damage that has been caused to the earth they now inherit. We hand the guardianship of the globe to the next generation at our peril, if we do so without offering parallel education and training in environmental protection. For it is this process that can help that generation to guide the world safely into the next century, and to seek the tools to undo environmental damage and ensure that the earth is a safe and healthy place for them to live and to prosper.

The future of the environment, and ultimately therefore of the human race, hangs very much in the balance at the present time. What the contributors to this volume all bring to this challenge is a common understanding that we must work on this challenge together, for it cannot be solved in any other way. So, in welcoming this initiative and encouraging its opening of doors to further companion projects I leave the last word to the Scottish Philosopher David Hume, and draw strength from his vision when he wrote:

It is a sense of shared humanity and that alone which can provide the basis for civilised existence. Though this affection of humanity may not generally be esteemed so strongly as vanity or ambition, yet being common to all men it can alone be the foundation of morals or and general system of blame or praise.

I hope this volume receives the success that it merits.

Part I - Introduction

Environmental Education and Training: an Introductory Essay

Patricia D Park
Chair of Law Research Centre, Southampton Institute

Gin Chong
Research Leader, Southampton Business School, Southampton Institute

The traditional areas of concern for modern peoples have been security, trade and economics; but the recent breakup of the bipolar world has freed intellectual energy and resources to meet new challenges. Within this new political context the opportunity exists for a dialogue on issues that touch on long-term environmental security. The demand for environmental knowledge and assessment continues to grow and in response the international agencies have set up successful programmes. By comparison how can all this knowledge be translated into positive action? To try to find some answers to this question, at least in part, a conference was arranged to take place in 1995. For various reasons this did not happen but the research papers submitted and the invited speakers produced ideas that should not be lost. Their words serve to do all the things that Professor Hughes hoped that the conference would do in provoking discussion, setting agendas and in some cases suggesting some of the answers to the various questions raised.

Most of the articles in this book outline the importance of an interdisciplinary approach to environmental regulation and education and why it is so important to bring other disciplines into the analysis of environmental law. Environmental regulation is necessarily an interdisciplinary activity which requires the bridging of several distinct fields; science, engineering, business management and the law, but all within the context of the inevitable financial constraints. This is because environmental regulation is concerned with the management of social interactions within the context of natural resource systems. In order to accomplish so broad a task it is an absolute necessity that co-operation is forged across disciplines.

Finance and management play an analogous role in the regulation of human societies to that which natural scientists do in the regulation of natural resources. Just as natural resource systems respond in complex ways to human intervention, human societies also respond in complicated ways to governmental intervention. It is then the role of the educator to describe the link between cause and effect within society that natural scientists draw in relation to nature. This base of understanding is then combined with the requisite legal and scientific knowledge in order to create an interdisciplinary framework capable of managing human interaction within natural resource systems.

The manner in which environmental law and regulation manifests itself when introduced within society can be as complex as the manner in which intervention manifests itself when introduced into the environment. These impacts must be carefully thought out and considered; otherwise entirely non-obvious or unintended responses may result. It is necessary for analysts of societal responses to be involved in the team that is preparing environmental legislation, if that legislation is to have the desired effect. All those interested in the creation of effective and meaningful environmental regulation should be interested in advancing this interdisciplinary approach to environmental law-making.

The acknowledgement of the part that advanced education has to play in informing opinion and stimulating debate about environmental issues has been well articulated in the international declaration in which University presidents or vice chancellors and principals in the United Kingdom stated their intention to take action to focus university attention on environment, population and development issues. The fact that it was supported by presidents from countries other than the United Kingdom who were amongst the initial signatories to the Declaration should not detract from the understanding that most British Universities would support the general proposition.

The relationship between 'Environmental Problems' and the part that the law has to play in the protection of the environment is discussed in some length by William Howarth; one conclusion being "the task is that of distinguishing the environmentally desirable from the environmentally compellable, and within the environmentally compellable the assignation of a gravity of compulsion". The role of academic environmental lawyers being to define and redefine the nature of the problem rather than taking the answer directly from other disciplines. The problem of the lack of any human legal right to a decent environment can be set against the man on the top of the Clapham omnibus who exclaims that 'there ought to be a law against it', concluding with the lawyers task being to analyze the nature of the issue needing to be addressed and assessing what kind of legal response is most appropriate.

The role of legal education is outlined as one which must address both theoretical and practice based environmental issues, but the range and complexity of recent primary and secondary legislation enacted on a diversity of environmental topics highlights the technical depth and breath of the subject. This begs the question as to the level of detail which needs to be imparted.

The Toyne Report, *Environmental Responsibility, An Agenda for Further and Higher Education*, (1993) suggests that value judgements should be 'given a wide berth' and Howarth gives the lawyerly response that "A reasoned and factual argument based on clearly articulated premises is more likely to influence value judgements than preaching", with the *caveat* that there is no harm introducing students to extremes of environmental values so long as there is no endorsement of any particular set of environmental values. It is the properly informed concern about environmental values together with the intellectual skills learned in an environmental law course which provides a lasting benefit to the student. As far as non-lawyers are concerned it is the intellectual rigour and the use of legal reasoning which introduces the non-lawyer to a distinct and different perspective of environmental issues and possible resolutions of environmental problems.

Significantly, the *Toyne Report's* focus on professional influences being brought to bear on higher education has come at a time when widespread concerns have been expressed, not just in Britain but internationally, about the form and nature of university undergraduate accounting education. In particular, degree programmes have come under increasing criticism for their emphasis on technical and calculative concerns together with their failure to develop questioning and analytical attitudes on the part of accounting students, or to foster an awareness of the social functioning of accounting practices. One acclaimed result of such processes is that a breed of accountants has been produced who are unable to adapt to changing economic and social circumstances, of which recent increasing public awareness of environmental issues is but one example, and hence lack the attributes of a true professional (Gay *et al*, (1994), *Accounting Education,* vol. 3, pp.51-75). The need is to expose students to material that fundamentally addresses the social and ethical functioning of the professions and acknowledges that the social and environmental issues are a contested and ever changing domain.

Education in social and environmental issues would seem to represent a prime mechanism for starting to address such a need at undergraduate level. They have been seen, amongst other things, to offer the potential for challenging traditional perspectives and to force students to clarify their own ethical standpoints and develop a deeper understanding of the extent to which their own profession is implicated in the process of social and political control.

The emergence over the last twenty years of an identifiable strand of research concerned with environmental issues has provided a ready educational basis for such teaching. Although there has been a recognised increase in legal environmental education, at both undergraduate and postgraduate level, there is little evidence concerning the coverage of social and environmental accounting issues in university accounting curricula, the impact of such teaching and the problems encountered by those attempting to develop it. Such a state of affairs with its suggestion of an apparent mismatch between claimed pedagogic advantage and practical development, provides the central motivation for a general re-examination of the objectives of undergraduate accounting education.

Unfortunately, one of the greatest obstacles to putting any type of creativity modules into undergraduate programmes with a strong vocational base is the professional examination priority in the minds of the students, professors and recruiters. Students who target, as a primary goal, the passing of the professional core exams have little time, interest and inclination to be sidetracked from what they see as the essential steps on the ladder to becoming a qualified professional in their chosen field. The result is that students may not be sufficiently exposed to conceptual material until later in their degree, by which time the mechanistic nature, particularly of accounting, has taken root and the ability to introduce alternative approaches is limited as it is met with resistance. More importantly, final year courses tend to offer students subject choice in a way which means that many will never be exposed to the type of material covered in environmental courses. This analysis begs the question as to whether students have been through an appropriate academic and 'mind broadening' experience after three years of university study or whether courses have merely pandered to students' expectations of a vocational degree as a preliminary and thus perceived necessary stage of professional training. Of course, in an era where higher education policy is being driven by notions of the student as customer, or consumer, of educational services, students' perceptions as to what is 'appropriate' university education are not something that can be dismissed lightly. However, the notion of the 'student as customer' is not unproblematic, particularly when it is recognised that opportunities for graduates to enter into professional training are rapidly shrinking. With such a decline in professional training vacancies having occurred during a period of rapid expansion in the numbers entering undergraduate education, one must surely fundamentally question the continuing dominance of the core curriculum predicated on the assumption that the majority of graduates will enter professional training. Nevertheless the aim must be to prepare students *to become professionals* not to be professionals at the time they enter the profession. The expanded knowledge base makes it impossible for new graduates to have the full range of knowledge and skills expected of the professional in practice. To be successful, all professionals must continue to learn and adapt to change throughout their careers. Pre-entry education should lay the basis on which lifelong learning can be built. As such, the focus should be on learning to learn. Talking of which, the exploring of underlying concepts and principles has a certain undoubted attraction, potentially offering the scope for university educators to explore issues that the previous devotion to techniques had prevented. Undergraduate studies could be firmly rooted in notions of social science and environmental awareness, and fundamentally seek to address the significance of the role and functioning of professional practice in society, especially their role in national and international processes of resource allocation and control. Ironically, this could enable (particularly accounting) degrees to secure a new, and more socially meaningful 'relevance' in an era when social ramifications and public policy implications are coming under increasing scrutiny.

Such an alternative perspective, within which environmental courses should play a key role, would also benefit those graduates still entering professional training. With a new and broader understanding of law and accounting these trainees surely would be much better equipped to critically appraise current practice and respond to new (or even old but unfulfilled) societal expectations; in fact, to exhibit the attributes of a true 'professional'. Current degrees, whose core content appears to be largely watered down versions of the professional syllabus do not achieve this end.

In a more specific area concerning the dissemination of knowledge, John Steel highlights a survey that concluded "although nine out of ten farmers agreed that the prevention of water pollution through the safe handling of pesticides, slurry and silage was important, very few of them were open to the idea that they needed more advice". Thereby lies a fundamental problem. How do the regulators fulfil the policy of co-operation with potential polluters rather than coercion, if the regulated are reluctant to take advice? The research also established that more than half of British farmers were not even aware of the official codes of good agricultural practice on environmental protection. Clearly, education about, and dissemination of the codes must be a first step before enforcement can be contemplated.

Education of environmental issues is a two way process. The education of the farmers and the dissemination of good practice on environmental protection is really only half of the story. The other half is the basis on which any further consideration is given to new regulation of agricultural activity. A fundamental concern of many commentators is that the move towards further regulation is based on inadequate research and knowledge; for example the statutory maximum admissible concentration of nitrates in drinking water was challenged by the Royal

Commission on Environmental Pollution in its 16th Report on Freshwater Quality in 1992 when it remained unconvinced that the strict limit imposed by the European Community Directive 80/68 was "..needed to protect health in the UK or any other country with a satisfactory public water supply system". The impact of phosphorus input from agriculture on the eutrophication of UK waters is another issue which, it is claimed, needs further research on behalf of the regulators. Once the research has been carried out to establish the level of risk of any given polluting activity, then education of the public is essential for the acceptance by the public of the newly established levels of permitted emissions.

John Steel puts forward the thesis that further regulation based on inadequate scientific knowledge and a sound risk assessment will be less effective in the protection of the environment than the education of farmers in good environmental management. This could be achieved by educating the farmers and the dissemination and enforcement of the codes of practice. This focus has been supported by the Advisory Committee on Business and the Environment (ACBE) in its sixth progress report, in recommending that the government should alter the remit of the Agricultural Training Board (ATB), putting more emphasis on promoting training and supporting the infrastructure of local training groups. A continuing problem, however, is the poor take-up of training courses by farmers. If farmers could be persuaded to take advantage of such initiatives they could make a significant contribution to reducing the impact that agricultural activities have on the environment.

Not only in the agricultural industry is there awareness of the need for educating the main players. The ACBE have also recognised that the recent debates surrounding environmental issues have highlighted the need for greater public understanding of the different issues involved in environmentally sensitive decision-making. ACBE members have held discussions with Sir Ron Dearing, Chairman of the Schools curriculum and assessment Authority, on the interaction between economic activity and the environment in the hope that business will co-operate in preparing materials to assist young people to develop their own understanding of environmental issues.

Informing the public and improving their understanding of the influences of the environment on their health will serve to enable people to improve the areas of the environment over which they have control and assist them in making informed choices about their lifestyle.

It is not only the industrialised world where the lack of knowledge of environmental issues and their regulation has an effect on the public good. Any industrial activity necessarily has a polluting effect on the environment to a greater or lesser degree and the need for knowledge of environmental issues and their regulation is effectively discussed in the papers included in this book. The final paper gives another perspective from a developing country, on the need for knowledge and how effective a group of people can be when armed with knowledge through education and understanding of the issues involved.

The paper gives an account of how a small group of dedicated environmentalists organized a campaign to force a public review of the adverse environmental impacts of a major development, which subsequently led to the projects disapproval. This is essentially a "David and Goliath" story with the requisite happy ending; but nevertheless is a shining example of what can be achieved by a group of knowledgable people who by educating the local

5

community as to the environmental issues at stake and also their rights under the legislation forced a biased government to think again.

All of the papers in this collection address different aspects of the need for environmental education. This is not restricted to the legal field, there being a strong argument for an interdisciplinary approach in order that lawyers and regulators have an all-round knowledge. Environmental education *per se* should not be restricted to undergraduates in institutions of higher education but the proposition that there is a need for both regulators and the regulated as well as the general public at large to have a thorough knowledge of environmental issues, including the law, is irrefutable. This list should also include the legislators. Without the proper knowledge and understanding, based on good verifiable research, on which the legislators can rely when promulgating new regulations or standards, those new regulations will not be acceptable to or accepted by the regulated and will inevitably lead to legal challenge.

Knowledge is power. With knowledge of the law and rights and duties under the law 'David' can show 'Goliath' the error of his ways, with the main beneficiary being the environment.

Back in the industrialized world, a business's environmental standing is becoming incresingly significant in terms of its overall performance and valuation. The financial sector, as an interested stakeholder, has an important role to play in helping to raise environmental standards, for example by encouraging business to improve its risk management. In this context current environmental reporting and accounting practices currently provides insufficient relevant information to allow financial analysts and fund managers make fully informed judgements of the businesses they are scrutinising.

Various scientific findings (for example effects on the ozone layer and dramatic climatic changes) indicated huge extent of human threats to the environment, not only regionally but to the global ecosphere. In society, awareness of environmental issues has been rising dramatically during the last twenty odd years, and environmental pressure group membership has been growing, in number as well as support, in most countries (Cairncross, 1991)[1]. This

---

[1]   National membership of environmental protection organisations compiled by Cairncross (1991) (in '000):

	1975	1980	1985	1990
Audubon Society (USA)	255	310	425	515--
Greenpeace (USA)	6	80	450	2000
National Wildlife Federation (USA)	2600 [1970]	4600	4500	5800
Sierra Club (USA)	153	182	363	566
Friends of the Earth (UK)	5	20 [1981]	30	200
National Trust (UK)	539	1047 [1981]	1323	2000
Royal Society for Nature Conservation (UK)	107	143 [1981]	166	250

awareness has brought in great demand for more environmental-friendly products by consumers, while forcing business organisations to modify their strategies and products (and services) to meet these increasing needs. All these have great impact on business organisations that it is worth paying to become 'green' or would otherwise be financially hurt or eventually be eliminated in the competitive world. Increasing the environmental performance of a business organisation could generate many benefits. These benefits could be either tangible that is improving sales and profits, or intangible for an example improving employee morale and better corporate image. However, business organisations cannot go on generating these benefits without any attached price tag. These are costs and/or liabilities.

Modern managers are increasingly concerned about the level of environmentally induced financial costs, and attempting to implement sustainable managerial and financial practices. However, environmentally induced opportunities and threats, costs and revenues, assets and liabilities are not normally explicitly reflected in companies' financial statements. It is time for accountants to report the environmental impact in the financial statements. We understand that this is not an easy task to the financial reporters, but they should work closely with experts of other disciplines (like engineers, environmental assessors) as to how best to estimate and report these environmental matters.

In order to achieve this, accountants themselves need to be educated. In the past, costs induced by ecological issues were neglected because it is not cost benefit to collect and report them. But now, the impact on the corporate image, the sense of social responsibilities, and the liabilities of failing to report these costs and liabilities could be detrimental to the survival of a business organisation (Gray, Bebbington and Walters, 1993). Proper environmental accounting systems need to be installed to capture, collate, analyse and to report this information in the financial statements.

It becomes an urgent need for all companies (both big and small) to set up a proper and reliable environmental accounting system to deal with activities, methods and systems for recording, analysing and reporting environmentally induced financial and ecological impact to the economic system (which includes a firm, region, or country) (Bebbington, Gray, Thompson, Walter 1994). This system should be capable of capturing needed information, financial or otherwise, for reporting to both internal and external users. These users or stakeholders are groups or individuals who have a stake in the business organisation. In order for these stakeholders to understand and fully appreciate the needs to report these environmentally induced costs and liabilities in the financial statements, it is essential that these groups are given the opportunities to learn and be educated on how to interpret these results, and have the ideas to translate these results into the extent of impact in their daily life. Financial statements should be kept simple and free from financial jargon. Bases of arriving the costs and liabilities should be disclosed in the financial statements. Items which have impact on environment, whether they are current or contingent, need to be highlighted.

It is the aim of this book to highlight the importance of educating not only the accountants on how these environmentally induced financial costs are reported, but also the general public as a whole. Accountants need to set up proper management accounting systems to capture relevant data which may have implications for the business organisations (Hrisak, 1995). These data need to be analysed carefully and reported to management for internal decision-making. All items having material impact on the decision making process of stakeholders (including shareholders, employees, lenders and general public) need to be separately disclosed in the financial statements accompanied with proper notes to the accounts explaining the impact and implications of all the reported information. It is worthwhile for accountants reporting (despite high costs) environmentally induced items to stakeholders as and when these items take place, rather than accumulating them and reporting at the financial year end. These will not only greatly assist stakeholders to make appropriate financial decisions as and when the reports were made available, but would also project the business organisation as a socially responsible unit in the society. In the long run, costs of reporting will become negligible as the benefits (both tangible and intangible) derived from prompt and accurate reporting will outgrow the costs.

To achieve all the above, accountants themselves need to be educated and properly trained as to how best to collect, collate and report this information to stakeholders (Harte and Owen, 1991). Apart from training the accountants, the accounting profession, either by itself or jointly with other professions like legal and management, should conduct continuous training sessions, seminars and workshops to educate the stakeholders. Only with these would the stakeholders would be able to appreciate and make use of these long-forgotten but important facts which have to be disclosed in the financial statements. The differences between fear of reporting (by accountants) and the expectations on reporting more (by stakeholders) will gradually diminish once all the groups are properly educated.

As far as environmental auditors are concerned, they need to process an appropriate level of auditing knowledge to discharge their duties. These include auditing, and analysing of both the financial and non financial information supplied by the management. These environmental auditors need to undergo appropriate levels of training and education. Apart from knowing the nature of business of the clients, they need to know and make themselves aware of the types of chemicals and waste which have or may have potentialities in damaging the environment, and external factors like legislative requirements. They need constantly to update their technical and professional knowledge, and be capable of communicating with their clients using jargon-free language on the importance of caring and maintaining the level of operations within the regulated boundary. Like managers, auditors need to be proactive in their approaches in the audit techniques. The audit procedures and techniques need to be reviewed constantly in line with the current and possibly forthcoming allowed legislative limits, and expected needs of the society.

In the course of an environmental audit, in view of the limitations on the scope of education and training, and high demands of specialists' knowledge, the environmental auditors may need to obtain specialists' opinions or even to work hand in hand with other specialists. These specialists include chemical consultants, assessors of land and properties, health and safety experts, environmental lawyers, and maritime engineers. It becomes necessity a for these environmental auditors to learn and master jargons which may not have been learned in their formal education. They need to attend various environmentally related seminars and conferences (not necessarily accounting or auditing-based seminars or conferences), and keep abreast with technical development by reading professional and journal articles.

The increasing demand on accounting and non aooounting knowledge on accountants and auditors look set for implementation of inter-disciplinary teaching ourriculums at all levels of educational institutions. Students are expected to know the basic environmental needs and protection, and as they advance to a higher level of education, they need to be taught how specialists in other disciplines work and discharge their professional duties. This type of inter-disciplinary training will increase the scope of exposure and knowledge of individuals when he or she are given the tasks of accounting and environmental audit process in the future.

Legislative needs and expectations, not only within the UK and the European Union, but also in a global perspective should be emphasised in the syllabi at schools. The idea of 'thinks globally, acts locally' should be instilled in everyone's mind, in particular to children of all ages. Education should not start at schools, it should commence even at home. Parents themselves should set good examples of how the environment should be taken care of, and constantly remind their children of the importance of caring for the surroundings which are meant for generations to come.

Accountants and auditors should be proactive in their approaches to the issue of environment. Apart from emphasising the importance of having environmental issues in their accounting syllabi, accounting bodies should constantly remind their members to serve their clients, management, and reporting to stakeholders on the importance of caring for environment. An accounting framework on environmental issues needs to be formulated, and the framework needs to focus on not only the current needs but also the future expectations. The framework should cover the issues of international as well as the local needs and expectations.

References

Bebbington, J., Gray, R., Thompson, I. and Walter, D. (1994), "Accountants' attitudes and environmentally sensitive accounting" *Accounting and Business Research*; vol. 24, no. 4; pp. 109-120.

Cairncross, F. (1991), *Costing the Earth. What governments must do. What consumers need to know. How business can profit*. London; Great Britain Books.

Department of The Environment and Department of Trade and Industry (1996), *Sixth Progress Report to and Response from the President of the Board of Trade and the Secretary of State for the Environment*; Advisory Committee on Business and the Environment; April 1996.

Department of Health and Department of The Environment (1996), *Consultative Document on The Environment and Health*; Department of Health and Department of The Environment; 1996.

Gray, R., Bebbington, J. and Walter, D. (1993), *Accounting of the Environment*. London; The Chartered Association of Certified Accountants.

Harte, G. and Owen, D. (1991), "Environmental disclosure in the annual reports of British Companies: a research note" *Accounting, Auditing and Accountability Journal*; vol. 4; No 3; pp.51-61.

Hrisak, D.M. (1995), "The bottom line is green" *Financial Forum*; vol. 4; no. 3; April, 1995; p.7.

Lord Chancellor's Advisory Committee (1996), *Consultation Paper on Continuing Professional Development*; The Lord Chancellor's Advisory Committee on Legal Education and Conduct; July 1996.

The Toyne Report, *Environmental Responsibility, An Agenda for Further and Higher Education*, (1993).

1   Environmental Legal Education - For Whom?

D J Hughes
Professor of Housing and Planning Law De Montfort University

The purpose of this paper is very much to ask questions, to provoke discussion, and to set agendas.

If I ask questions perhaps some of the answers are already present - let us at least hope so. Let us also hope that the questions make sense, for nothing is more futile than the apparently deep and profound question to which there can be no sort of answer. Such a question is far too often designed only to achieve one object: to keep everyone in an impotent state of ignorance while they search for an answer that cannot be given.

If I provoke discussion - may be even mildly heated disagreement (I expect restraint from my audience) - then that is excellent; it is exactly what the organisers of this symposium volume asked me to achieve.

If I set agendas - ah, then I *will* have achieved something, for let us remember that an "agendum" is something to be done, and if I send my readers on fired and determined to do something constructive, then I shall feel proud that I have not merely added to global warming by consuming too many trees by way of paper.

The mention of global warming brings me back quite properly to do what it is I am supposedly dealing with - legal education about the environment - who it is for, and how we are to further its advancement and improvement.

I do not expect to come to any very definite conclusions about this - nor would it be wise to do so - let us remember that the International Standards Office (ISO) has yet to formulate an internationally acceptable definition of what the environment is - and it would surely be wrong to reach conclusions before the ISO!

Allow me, please to begin by posing an initial question. How prominent are lawyers in the United Kingdom in environmental matters? Now lawyers reading this may say "we have the United Kingdom Environmental Law Association" - an excellent organisation it is too, and I for one am proud to have been a founder member. Practitioner lawyers will say "we have a very large number of most prestigious firms who conduct a considerable amount of business for major clients world wide, while there are other excellent and committed firms only too willing to nip and harry the heels of major companies and undertakings when they transgress the law, and to seek justice for those who allege they have suffered as a result of maltreatment of the environment". Academic lawyers will say "we have excellent courses on offer - well over 1000+ undergraduates study the subject each year - we have a number of high prestige postgraduate degrees, yes and we have several leading and well thought of text books dealing with matters legal and environmental".

These are not answers to my question. They simply describe a response made by lawyers to perceived needs, and while excellent in their own way, no doubt, they do not necessarily mean that lawyers are particularly prominent in environment policy making. I believe in fact that lawyers are not particularly central to decision making on environmental issues. Look at two of the most influential environment bodies, The Royal Commission on Environmental Pollution and The Environment Agency which has recently had its membership announced. Amongst the membership of those two august bodies lawyers, *on the whole*, are more conspicuous by their absence than by their presence: *Why*?

When I was a postgraduate student my supervisor argued on one occasion when we met that in general lawyers in the UK do not become involved centrally in matters of policy and administrative regulation until it is too late, ie. until the form and content of the particular policy and its attending implementing legislation and regulations have become relatively fixed. Once the legal structure is in place, of course, the lawyers will come in to argue about vires and locus standi and Wednesbury unreasonableness, etc, etc, etc. But by then the influence of the lawyer will be comparatively minor and peripheral. All too often it is the case that the lawyer is a "johnny-come-lately" who is tacked on to the end of the policy and decision making process, but who has not been central to it.

This may be due to a long lingering, post Dickensian malodour clinging to lawyers; it may be due to a perception that lawyers are quite simply only "in it for the money"; it may be because lawyers are thought of as being merely negative and destructive, only concerned to restrict and hedge about the operation of the law so that their particular clients can get on with making profit - in this present context at the environment's expense. No doubt there is some truth in all of these points of view, but my own feeling is that the most important reason for the marginalisation of lawyers in environmental matters is because of problems of language, communication and understanding - *and that is an educational issue*.

If we pause to consider each of the disciplines relevant to an understanding of the issues that affect the environment we must soon realise that each has its own vocabulary and linguistic conventions. Furthermore even where those disciplines use words in common those words may in fact have very different meanings according to the particular context, and in relationship to the particular discipline using them. I return here to my earlier allusion to the ISO; that body has yet to draw up a single comprehensive definition of the concept of "the environment" acceptable to all its member states - and the work of coming to an acceptable definition is expected to take at least another two years. A similar timescale applies to defining many other terms in regular use in environmental circles. On the other hand we can often encounter situations where a lawyer and an environmental scientist may each be talking about an observable phenomenon in words which mean nothing, or very little, to the other person in the conversation. Take for example a release of some chemical compound into water. The lawyer will be concerned very much with whether this is "poisonous, noxious or polluting" - high sounding words but ones with little meaning to, for example, the chemist, who is much more concerned with notions of "toxicity".

It is this problem of vocabulary and communication that I feel we must address; not just so that lawyers can become more involved in environmental issues, but to ensure that legal regulation takes place in a sensible and workable fashion which has paid due heed to the methods, principles and teachings of the natural, social and economic sciences, and which does not require those who are regulated to achieve that which is scientifically impossible. Put it another way: lawyers need to become more involved at an early stage when an environmental issue is identified as one requiring some form of regulation in order to bring into play their particular skills in deciding whether the matter is one susceptible of *legal* regulation, and, if so, what the most appropriate form of regulation will be.

There are, I suggest, three ways at least in which this problem can be addressed, and I would like to put each in the form of questions particularly pertinent to the world of higher education.

1) Are we gathering together in centres of environmental excellence teams of, eg, scientists, economists and lawyers whose common research aim is to seek the best and most effective means of environmental protection and regulation?

2) Are we undertaking the creation of new sorts of degree course in which we are producing graduates who can cross at least two disciplinary boundaries and who have a degree of fluency in more than one appropriate "language" so that they may act as channels of communication between others who have pursued, perhaps in a more specialised way, only one of the relevant disciplines?

3) Where are the books to explain environmental law and regulation to scientists; more particularly as a lawyer let me ask, where are the books to explain the environmental sciences to lawyers?

Let me address these issues in turn.

When we consider the natural sciences, and the way in which their study is organised in universities, we would conclude that an individual who attempted to conduct an entire research programme alone could be at best ill advised, and, at worst, possibly paranoid and incapable of meaningful contact and discussion with others. This is not to say, of course, that there are not individual discoveries and individual initiative, but on the whole the picture that comes to mind when we think of a research laboratory is of groups of people working together - some as leaders, some as postdoctoral fellows, some as research students etc, etc. The published nature of scientific papers shows how in general they are the product of team effort. Generally speaking universities would expect to *have* to gather together, and pay for, whole teams of scientific scholars if they wish to establish a name for themselves within a particular area of the natural sciences.

But that is not the case with academic environmental lawyers. One person may be expected to be the academic concerned to conduct both teaching and research in the legal aspects of environmental concerns - maybe having to teach not just his/her own LLB undergraduates and postgraduates, but having to undertake a service teaching for other departments who believe their students could benefit from a little "legal input".

It is not my brief, nor even my concern, to criticise individual institutions but there are places - some of them universities who would be in any one's top ten, fifteen or thirty in research terms - where there are concentrations in depth of internationally acclaimed strength in environmental sciences - both the natural and the social - yet where the law school either has only one person known to be "research active" in environmental law or has no one professing an interest in the specialism. In one university I can think of there is an outstanding concentration of relevant natural and social scientific expertise in the environmental area: there is, however, no law school. Not that I am saying we need yet another law school, but the existence of that one, perhaps idyllic, place does indicate, at least, something of a mismatch of resources.

What I call for is not for individual colleagues in individual departments to get together and discuss joint research projects - laudable and worthwhile though that undoubtedly is. Nor is it for the production of pan-university volumes in which all the skills and research interest of those claiming an interest in environmental matters are recorded, even though that is a useful and important exercise. What I seek as an essential matter is a culture within universities that seeks to bring together *from the top down* collections of specialists from the range of relevant environmental disciplines, including the law. That cultural commitment must also accept that each relevant expert cluster must have strength in depth and numbers if truly effective joint research programmes are to be developed and pursued. Not every university will be able or willing to achieve this, nor would it be essential, or possible, for the numbers of participants in each collaborating unit to be equal, but I nevertheless believe that if even a comparatively small number of universities gathered together numbers of scholars in the way I have outlined the result would be the emergence of true centres of environmental excellence in an "across the board" fashion.

Some such gatherings have happened - one suspects somewhat fortuitously - in the past, but I cannot think of any that has survived long term. There are signs of hope - the translation of Professor Richard Macrory to Oxford to head the Climate Change Group, and the continued commitment of his erstwhile institution, Imperial College, to encouraging the presence of lawyers amongst the scientists are both causes for that hope. However, I believe we need more, much more, than this.

Let me now turn to the topic of the degree courses we offer and ask whether they are particularly apt to foster that bringing together of the various involved disciplines in meaningful debate and mutual support.

There is one initial question I must ask to which, I will admit, I have no current answer. That is: should connections be made solely at the postgraduate level or are new ventures required for undergraduates? At the postgraduate level there are a number of different types of course which can enable the building of bridges between disciplines and in which law is an element to a greater or lesser extent. For example in my own current institution we have the very well established MA in Environmental Law which has been so designed that it is capable of being undertaken by non-lawyers - and so far it has been successfully undertaken by, inter alia, an environmental health officer, a town planner, a plant ecologist, a mechanical engineer, a water planner, an environmental consultant and a marine biologist - oh yes, and by a lot of lawyers as well! At my former institution, the University of Leicester, there is the MSc in Natural Resource Management which for the past six years has attracted home based and international students to study law, principles of conservation, economics, remote sensing, microbial ecology and a number of other relevant topics - tough going and not for the faint hearted, but, again, attractive to a number of students from a very wide range of backgrounds. No doubt the examples of such postgraduate degrees can be multiplied, and, without any doubt, such programmes have a very important part to play in bringing relevant disciplines together. The problem is that, like all postgraduate programmes, such degree courses are not cheap to put on.

So could anything be achieved at the somewhat cheaper undergraduate level? This is where I can only step tentatively, where I can only set up a number of Aunt Sallys for others to knock down if they can and will. However, let me put this forward as an idea. It should be possible to assemble within a modular framework a number of cognate modules which, if taken in series, should enable a student, whose major subject is one of the natural or social sciences relevant to environmental regulation and protection, eg. chemistry or economics, to gain a sufficient insight into the nature and functioning of law to enable that person, say in employment, to act as a bridge between others. Consider a person with a degree primarily in chemistry, whose wish is to become an operational manager within the chemical industry, and who is particularly well qualified to interface with both "pure" scientists and "pure" lawyers because he/she has received specialised legal tuition at undergraduate level.

At the moment - and I stand open to correction here - we may be doing this simply by allowing students from the natural/social sciences to take a few law modules, perhaps the environmental law module, from the existing law programme. I know of universities where that takes place: but I believe it should not. To expect a student who has spent, let us say, two years studying Chemistry to then pick up more than an incomplete smattering of knowledge by studying environmental law for one quarter of his/her final year seems to me to be an over sanguine hope. We do not, after all, expect students to be all that knowledgeable about their various disciplines even at the end of their second year - and I will defend that proposition by pointing to the very considerable improvement in performance which most students demonstrate in their third year as their knowledge and understanding of their disciple deepens and matures. I am therefore not in favour of a "pick and mix" approach which pitches the uninitiated natural scientist straight into the mysteries of unravelling exactly what is was the Lord Chancellor was trying to achieve as he considered the meaning of "cause or knowingly permit" in the most recent Yorkshire Water case. No, I put forward the notion of degrees which, from a legal professional point of view are non-qualifying, and which contain a number of specially selected modules to introduce students to, and to staircase them through, law making procedures, legal systems, and legal processes as a proper foundation for the study of environmental law - the whole object being *not* to produce quasi lawyers but people who can sensibly, quickly and intelligibly interface with lawyers in a professional context.

So the question I leave for you here is whether any university can say it is actually doing this at the moment, or whether there are institutions willing to take the risk and to commit the resources to development of this type of degree programme?

Finally, and very briefly, where are the multi-disciplinary teams who are going to produce the "interface" books to enable meaningful interdisciplinary dialogue to take place? I can claim some modest participation in such a venture as I am part of the team which produces the Royal Society of Chemistry's volume "Understanding Our Environment". However, one type of book I believe to be needed and currently lacking is a work to explain basic principles of environmental science to lawyers. The two longest cases on record in English Civil Courts both concerned environmental issues. The *Hope and Reay* case concerned litigation against BNFL in respect of alleged genetic damage of fathers giving rise to subsequent cancers amongst their children, while the *Graham* case concerned an allegation of damage to cattle by emissions from a major incinerator plant operated by Rechem. Having spoken to the learned judge who had to decide the first case, and the team of defence solicitors in the second I can say that they were unanimous that the most difficult task faced by all the lawyers was mastering the science involved and getting hold of some of the particularly difficult scientific concepts encountered.

We are beginning to find glossaries of scientific terms in legal environmental works - Richard Burnett-Hall's monumental work on the subject contains an excellent example. But, once again, I believe we need more than this - and I am sure we can have it. This is a generation in which we can, indeed we must, bring together all the expertise which exists in our universities to produce works of mutual elucidation, enlightenment and education. So therefore let me conclude with a final request. Will the teams prepared to undertake such work please step forward.

Endnote

This paper was originally written as a keynote address for a conference which was never held. However, the conference organisers as the editors of this volume have kindly requested the author to include it in the present volume. It has not been revised since it was written in 1995 and time has thus rendered its ancient truth uncouth in some ways. Professor Macrory's move to Oxford proved to be only an excursion, for instance. On a happier note, however, one notes the publication by the Doctors McEldowney of their excellent text on science, law and the environment (Longman 1996). No doubt there are also many institutions now planning exciting multi-disciplinary research work and degree programmes on environmental issues in which lawyers are fully involved - or are there?

2 The Essence of an Environmental Law Education

William Howarth
Cripps Harries Hall / SAUR (UK), Professor of Environmental Law, University of Kent at Canterbury

Comprehensive Challenge and Individual Contribution

Recent years have exposed the enormity, complexity and gravity of the environmental challenges confronting humanity and the urgency with which these must be practically addressed if the internationally proclaimed imperative of sustainable development is to be realised[1]. The almost universal consensus is that present demands upon the earth, the environmental media and the ecosystems which they support, cannot continue. Major changes must be made to patterns of production and consumption, use of resources and individual lifestyles, particularly in developed countries, if the decline is to be halted. Broadly, there is agreement about general objectives such as reducing pollution, consuming less non-renewable resources and minimising human impact upon biodiversity. The critical disputes are about strategy: what means are most appropriately pursued towards a given, if somewhat imprecisely defined, end point.

Proposed 'solutions' to the environmental challenge abound. Some would advocate greater technical advancement to abate pollution, others the reduction of energy and resource consumption, the control of population, the implementation of environmentally sensitive markets, the promotion of greater public awareness of environmental problems and appreciation of environmental ethics and responsibility. All of these, and others, have a place in meeting the challenge but, it is suggested, none of them alone is adequate. Such is the momentous nature of the task that all branches of human ingenuity must be brought to bear upon it. Anything less than a comprehensive response underestimates the magnitude of what is involved.

Having reaffirmed the fundamental premise that a multi-disciplinary and, to some extent, inter-disciplinary strategy is needed, the question may still be meaningfully asked, what contribution may particular disciplines make to this task? The purpose of this chapter is to ask that question in relation to environmental law: what can this subject contribute to the environmental challenge which cannot be contributed by the other specialisms involved, and how can education in environmental law maximise this contribution? Hence, the central issue to be addressed in this discussion concerns the *distinctive* contribution of environmental law to the collective endeavour and the approach to teaching the subject which will maximise that contribution.

Inevitably, many of the observations are based on experience and reflection on teaching environmental law over many years and are difficult to justify on the basis of 'hard' empirical evidence, but it is hoped that this impressionistic approach may be of some value. Also notable as a factor which has moulded the preconceptions of the author is his role as a teacher in a United Kingdom university law school. Others, based within different jurisdictions or different kinds of educational institution, may well choose to differ in their emphases on some of the fundamental issues. The danger is noted of extrapolating ones experiences beyond their legitimate limits but it is difficult to avoid this if anything of general relevance is to be offered!

The discussion commences with some observations about the role of general and specialist environmental education and is followed by an attempt to identify the essential features of environmental law which set it apart from other areas of specialist environmental study. Having provided at least a broad identification of the subject area and its subdivisions, some suggestions are offered as to what objectives may be sought in providing an environmental law education noting the differences in approach that may be needed and particularly the differences where student bodies are composed of law and non-law students. Critically, the balance between facts and values is a matter which all involved in environmental education must address and some observations are offered as to how this balance may be tackled in environmental law teaching.

Environmental Education and Environmental Law Education

To some extent education in environmental law shares some features with environmental education generally. At all levels of education, in almost all subjects, there has been a marked 'greening of the curriculum' over recent years. Largely this is perceived to be due to a recognition of an ethical imperative of stewardship,[2] which must be understood and appreciated by all as a part of the responsibility of citizenship. In order to appreciate our personal responsibilities towards the environment we must be better informed as to individual and collective impacts upon the environment and the consequences of these for present and future generations.

Alongside this progress in general environmental education there has been significant expansion in specialist knowledge about the environment, particularly in institutions of further and higher education. To some degree this is perceived to be meeting a demand for environmental practitioners of various kinds. In other respects it may be thought of as an acknowledgement that advanced education has a particular role to play in informing opinion and stimulating debate about environmental concerns. These concerns have been well articulated in the "The Talloires Declaration"[3]. This international declaration resolves that University presidents, or vice chancellors and principals in the United Kingdom, must take action to focus university attention on environment, population and development issues and, amongst other things, they should:

- use every opportunity to raise public, government, foundation and university awareness by publicly speaking out on the importance of environmental concerns;

- encourage outstanding scholars who engage in research and teaching on environmental topics, and help them lead other scholars in this direction;

- establish programs in all major disciplines to teach about environment, population and sustainable development in the context of these disciplines; and

- establish multidisciplinary and interdisciplinary structures, such as "centres of excellence" for research, education and policy development within the university.

Regrettably, there were no vice-chancellors or principals from United Kingdom universities amongst the initial signatories to the Declaration, but it was supported by presidents of universities from many represented countries. Arguably, the declaration represents an international feeling that universities have an increasingly important role to play in environmental matters, and it is likely that most British universities would support that general proposition.

Certainly, if the growth of specialist environmental education in British Universities is any indication, there is clear evidence of increasing weight being attached to environmental teaching and research of all kinds. Education in environmental law closely follows this trend but raises some special issues which are largely unique to its subject matter.

Environmental Law and 'Environmental Problems'

An unavoidable point of departure is with the identification of the subject matter of environmental law. This enquiry probably admits as many answers as there are environmental lawyers since it is apparent that many of them conceive of their task quite differently. International, European and national environmental lawyers sometimes seem to share little common ground as do those concerned with the law concerning distinct kinds of environmental problem. The question must be posed, however, what are the shared features to their activities which serve to distinguish them from other areas of law and environmental scholarship.

As good a suggestion as any is that environmental law is defined by its purposive dimension. That is, environmental law "means the law from many sources which can be called into play to cope with environmental problems"[4]. This is incontrovertibly true, and informative in drawing a contrast between other branches of the law such as contract, tort and crime which seem to admit more conceptually-based definitions. However, it leaves everything to turn upon the issue of what is an 'environmental problem' and, perhaps more fundamentally, *who* is capable of providing an appropriate answer to the question.

The answers seem to be multifarious. 'Self-evidence theorists' will tend to define environmental problems in terms of the kind of high-profile events which gain media recognition as such: oil tanker casualties, 'accidental' chemical emissions and 'unacceptable' hunting or exploitation of wildlife. 'Expert-deference theorists' will identify environmental problems with whatever is presently thought environmentally unacceptable by the scientific and technical community according to whatever (self-referential) standards that community stipulates. Anthropocentricists will identify environmental problems in terms of a level of adverse impact upon human beings, whilst ecocentricists will identify them in terms of level of impact on ecosystems and their (non-human) living constituents. Clearly, the different schools of thought will differ widely not only in their respective catalogues of 'environmental problems', but also on the fundamental basis upon which a particular matter should be included or excluded.

The flaws in each of these positions are fairly readily apparent when presented in this crude and unsympathetic fashion. Media orientation towards sensationalism has little time for more mundane issues closer to home whatever their cumulative environmental or ecological impact. Scientists and technicians are authoritative arbiters of science of technology but not of matters of value. Anthropocentric and ecocentric positions, at least in their pure form, rest upon distinct ethical positions which have a dubious claim to be representative, or even feasible in some instances.

Does the legal perception of an environmental problem offer any preferable alternative? From a legal *practitioner's* viewpoint, an environmental problem is likely to be defined in terms of any situation which is legally actionable (in International, European or national criminal or civil law) primarily because of an adverse impact upon environmental media or ecosystems, or because it infringes private rights in these. This raises many 'grey' issues as to whether a complaint is primarily environmental or of another kind, such as those concerned with the protection of property rights, the built environment, amenity and access, environmental health, animal welfare or other interfacing legal concerns. Views will differ as to what matters are *primarily* environmental, but it is suggested that some level of consensus is securable on the central concerns of the subject.

From an *academic* and educational environmental law perspective the concerns are less pragmatically defined. The concern is not merely to identify and describe the existing law concerned with protection of the environmental media and ecosystems, but also to investigate what environmental laws there could or *should* be and what form these laws should take. The evaluative dimension to this may require assessments of the adequacy of present laws from extra-legal perspectives of a technical, ethical or other kind, alongside more traditional approaches towards consistency or functionality within a legal system. Reasoned arguments that an environmental law is scientifically misconceived or meaningless, ethically indefensible, or simply non-existent, are all 'fair game' for an academic enquiry, though likely to be of only marginal significance to legal practitioners.

To some degree, the academic environmental lawyer's enterprise is unavoidably political in the sense that any evaluation, or argument for legal change, has a political dimension. This is not necessarily to align the exercise with any party-political position, but rather to evaluate environmental priorities and offer legal responses on the basis of a broad range of technical considerations and values and an intimate appreciation of how these may be incorporated into law.

Beyond that, it is suggested that the subjection of environmental laws (actual and possible) to academic analysis has a significant role to play in defining the nature and gravity of environmental problems. The exercise of drawing an inference that a matter *should* justifiably be the subject of a particular kind of legal control involves an evaluative synthesis of scientific and ethical concerns. The question at issue is no longer an abstract enquiry as to what is an environmental problem, but rather what environmental problems permit and require a legal response and what that response should be from amongst the range of legal options that are available. Put another way, the task is that of distinguishing the environmentally desirable from the environmentally compellable, and within the environmentally compellable the assignation of a gravity of compulsion.

Perhaps some of these tasks overlap with the roles of environmental politicians or legislators, but the difference is that academics advance ideas rather than a tangible end-point in the form of a party environmental policy or a piece of legislation. On occasions these ideas may be translated into a tangible legal form, but their measure is always in terms of academic rigour rather than in terms of practical implementation. A good academic argument is not diminished by the unpopularity (political or otherwise) of its conclusion.

There is a sense, therefore, in which academic environmental lawyers *do* define and redefine the nature of the problem rather than taking an answer 'off the peg' from other disciplines. Moreover, it is suggested that this is done in a way which is distinct from the approaches adopted by other disciplines. This must have important educational implications. Whilst many legal educators would probably make ill-informed teachers of environmental science, philosophy or economics, they have unrivalled expertise in teaching what is distinctively contributed to the environmental debate from their own discipline, albeit informed by others.

Subdivisions of Environmental Law

Turning, more specifically, to the content of environmental law, and without reiterating the points made above about differences of perspective between environmental lawyers, there are probably three general foci of attention:

1.   broadly-formulated environmental obligations that are internationally entered into between nations, and more detailed matters which are the subject of international law within the European Community and other convention-governed systems of regional international law;

2.   specified kinds of activity which have an adverse effect upon environmental media or ecosystems and may be subject to national criminal prohibition, licensing authorisation or civil liability; and

3.   the allocation of a range of administrative functions to international and national bodies responsible for the collaboration, co-ordination, regulation, implementation and enforcement of environmental policy or regulation.

In addition to these, there is increasing scope to encompass topics which interface with other areas of law but have a strong environmental dimension. Examples of this kind might be access to environmental information, environmental dimensions of trade-related regulation, legal structures for environmental business management and environmental insurance.

Within each of the subdivisions of environmental law, clearly, a body of substantive information has to be imparted by an educator. Beyond that, the elusive quality of appreciation has to be conveyed. The person in the street recognising an environmental problem may respond with the affirmation 'there ought to be a law against it'. The environmental lawyer appreciates that 'thou shalt be nice to the environment' may be a moral imperative, but is not capable of being an environmental law. The lawyers' task is that of precisely analysing the nature of the issue needing to be addressed and assessing what kind of legal response is most appropriate.

States which propose to enter into international environmental obligations must be informed as to the practical nature of their commitments and the implications of these for domestic legislation. If an action is to be made the subject of a criminal prohibition, it is necessary that the accused should know what behaviour is capable of constituting a crime and the crime defined with sufficient precision for a court to be able to determine exactly where the offence has been committed. Similarly, the civil law requires that rights and duties that may be the subject of civil proceedings are clearly defined. Likewise, administrative and regulatory bodies must be subject to clearly formulated constitutions precisely defining their powers and duties.

All of these are tasks in which the environmental lawyer has a unique role to play. The educator's role is to equip the environmental lawyer with the necessary knowledge, awareness and expertise to formulate environmental obligations with the precision which is required by the law and to inform or advise on the practical implications of these obligations.

The Role of the Environmental Law Educator

Many of the general objectives of an environmental law education are shared with other legal and non-legal disciplines: the coherent presentation of a body of information and methods; stimulation of an analytical appreciation of purpose and limitations of the subject; and encouragement of the capacity for critical awareness[5]. Beyond these, general intellectual skills, there is likely to be a significant emphasis placed upon the development of legal concepts drawn from other areas of law and applied to environmental contexts. Some of this may be of direct relevance to professional practice, other parts are more likely to be of a more theoretical character.

An unavoidable feature of law teaching in British university law schools is the inclination of a sizeable part of the student body towards legal practice. This is reflected in the fact that a major part of the law curriculum is devoted to the 'core' courses required for professional exemption. In many instances the numbers of students following subjects which are not perceived to be vocationally relevant are small. At a time when higher education is becoming increasingly subject to a "consumer culture",[6] it is difficult to overlook the outlook of students who have increasingly vocational aspirations. On the other hand, the need to provide an active (rather than passive) liberal education and for university law schools to avoid effective duplication of professional practice vocational education must also be weighed into the balance. Perceived relevance to legal practice should not be allowed solely to determine the content of the environmental law syllabus, or the approach towards teaching it, but it may be appropriate to recognise the respective practical and academic importance of the topics which are covered. Most importantly, a university level education in environmental law must provide the opportunity for students to challenge any aspect of the 'received wisdom' of the subject matter and for this to be recognised as an educational achievement.

A particular difficulty in teaching environmental law concerns the level of detail entered into. A brief glance at the range of recent primary and secondary legislation enacted on almost any environmental topic will suffice to convince anyone of the technical depth and breadth of the subject. An unavoidable question for the educator is the level of detail which needs to be imparted. Clearly, this will depend upon the specialisation of the course, but at a university level a conceptual bias is always justified even where this means that much of the minutia must be omitted as a consequence. No amount of time will ever allow a course to be fully "comprehensive" of all that could be said about environmental law. What is necessary is that the statement of objectives and content of the scheme of study should be accompanied by an explicit explanation of priorities so that students are left under no misapprehensions as to why emphasis has been placed upon particular topics with others being dealt with cursorily or omitted.

The Place of Environmental Values

More generally, value assumptions underlying a course of study on environmental law should be articulated to an extent that reflects their degree of controversiality. Whilst there is nothing academically objectionable about an ultra-radical or an ultra-conservative approach towards the subject, it is important that extremes of opinion are acknowledged and students informed that the approach that is being taken may be regarded as departing from the 'mainstream'. These are probably matters of professional ethics recognised by anyone involved in university teaching, but may become especially problematic for those involved in teaching environment-related subjects particularly in the social sciences. As the point was put in the *Toyne Report*:

> "there are values at the heart of the environmental agenda: and, as often where values are involved, there are differing views about the proper educational response. There are those who cast environmental education in an overtly evangelistic role; at the other end of the spectrum are those who see serious dangers of simplistic one-sidedness, unless environmental education gives values a wide berth and restricts itself to scientific issues".[7]

Clearly, the option of 'giving values a wide berth' is not available to those teaching environmental law, or any other area of law, but it is suggested that the sophistication of most law students in forming their own value judgments is such that excessive evangelism may well be counter-productive. A reasoned and factual argument based on clearly articulated premises is more likely to influence value judgements than preaching. Nevertheless, providing that matters of fact and value are recognised as such, there is no harm introducing students to extremes of environmental values so long as the eventual examination or assessment process requires only the capacity to provide an informed evaluation of matters of value, rather than the endorsement of any particular set of environmental values. As the *Toyne Report* concludes on this point:

> "insofar as education seeks to lead opinion, it will do so more effectively if it keeps in mind the distinctive nature of its mission, which is first and foremost to improve its students' *understanding*. Their *concern* may well be awakened as a result; but it must be a properly informed concern".

Awakening a properly informed concern about environmental values through the study of environmental law may be no bad thing but, again, the successful accomplishment of the exercise is better judged in terms of level of understanding of matters of fact and value that is conveyed (along with the other intellectual skills discussed above) rather than the strength of the emotions that are raised.

Environmental Law for Non-lawyers

Whilst most of the preceding discussion has tended to assume that the main recipients of environmental law teaching are law students, an increasing amount of environmental law teaching is being presented to students from non-law backgrounds. Science students from the whole spectrum of natural sciences, and particularly environmental science, are increasingly keen to have their subjects placed in practical, regulatory and administrative contexts. Likewise there are an increasing number of interdisciplinary schemes of study in 'environmental management' which seek to link social and natural scientific approaches to the environment with a particular emphasis upon increasing need for industries to direct attention to their environmental housekeeping. Whilst, in the past, many of these schemes of study have tended to be at postgraduate level, an increasing number of undergraduate opportunities are being provided for environmental management and related areas.

In relation to environmental law teaching to primarily non-law students, the question then arises how should the approach differ from the teaching of environmental law to law students? What is, say, an environmental science student reasonably expected to acquire from pursuing a course of study in environmental law? It is suggested that the answer is, a lawyer's insight into environmental processes of a kind that differs from those gained from other subjects that the student has already studied, or is studying. Clearly, there will be interrelationships between environmental law and other environmental subjects, in terms of the problems that are addressed. However, within an multidisciplinary context, it is the *distinctiveness* of environmental law, rather than its common feature of being an environmentally-related subject, which most contributes to its value to non-lawyers.

If environmental law is a distinctive-but-relevant subject for many kinds of non-law student, the problem remains as to how the distinction and relevance of environmental law is to be conveyed. The difficulty is that whilst teaching law students it may reasonably be assumed that the students will be possessed of a fair grasp of key legal concepts, this assumption may not be fairly made of students from a non-law background. Essentially, therefore, some work must be done in introducing students to the different kind of legal norm: international laws, European laws, criminal laws, licensing authorisations and civil liability, and the interrelations between these in a legal system. This need not be over-detailed, and can often be effectively accomplished by introducing examples from relevant environmental contexts rather than as abstract principles. Nevertheless, some background of this kind is unavoidable if more detailed matters of environmental regulation are to be coherently presented.

Thereafter, environmental law may often gain a particular relevance for non-law students by building upon the insights and aspirations of the students concerned. Perhaps they may relate to the law most directly by perceiving of themselves as an environmental manager of an industrial process or as the employee of an environmental regulatory authority. Providing that the approach does not become too one-sided there is much to be gained by putting environmental law into these kinds of context. Indeed, industrialist-versus-regulator perspectives are almost guaranteed to provide special relevance to broader debates about environmental values and serve to add a significant contextual background to other areas of study.

Notwithstanding all this, it is suggested that the limitations of environment law teaching to non-law students are not so different to those arising in relation to the teaching of law students. That is, that the distinctive contribution of the law is being emphasised, not to the diminution of other concerns, but by saying that the law has this to offer to the environmental challenge which confronts humanity. It amounts to only one facet of a much broader approach to the environmental challenge, but its integrity sets it apart from all others.

Concluding Observations

Drawing the threads together, the main inference is that environmental law has a vital role to play in meeting the environmental challenge and this role is of a unique kind which must be influential in determining how the subject is taught. The subject rests upon a combination of science and values but contributes a distinctive normative dimension which goes beyond either of these. Any suggestion that law serves merely to place an authoritative stamp on a prevailing orthodoxy of scientific thought or environmental values must be emphatically resisted.

The implications of this for teaching environmental law are readily apparent. Whilst the subject is informed by, and subject to evaluation from, the whole spectrum of environmental disciplines, its distinctive status should be recognised as such. Interdisciplinary or multidisciplinary teaching of environmental subjects should not be allowed to obscure differences of approach to the challenges involved. For both law students and non-law students a consciously new horizon should be made available.

Notes

(1)   see HMSO, *Sustainable Development the UK Strategy* (1994) Cm.2426.

(2)   see HMSO, *This Common Inheritance* (1990) Cm.1200 p.10.

(3)   *Report and Declaration of the [University] Presidents Conference* (1990).

(4)   Lyall, in Foreword to McManus, *Environmental Health Law in Scotland* (1989).

(5)   see Higher Education Quality Council discussion paper, *What are Graduates ?* (1996).

(6)   see Oliver, "The Integration of Teaching and Research in the Law Department" (1996) *The Law Teacher* 133.

(7)   Department for Education and Welsh Office, *Environmental Responsibility An Agenda for Further and Higher Education* (1993) p.22.

3 Reducing the Impact of Agriculture on Water Quality: Legal Controls or Education?

John Steel
Partner, White & Bowker, Solicitors

In 1988 the European Community issued Council Directive 88/708 for the protection of fresh coastal and marine waters against pollution caused by nitrates from diffuse sources. This Directive was targeted primarily at pollution by agriculture arising from land management practices, excessive land application of animals manures and over use of chemical fertiliser. It was felt necessary to control the input of nitrate to the aquatic environment and to achieve a maximum admissible concentration of 50 mg/l for drinking water.

Statistics were submitted by various European countries. From these statistics it appears possible to connect high levels of nitrate with intensity of agricultural activity. In Belgium the average nitrate content in the Ardennes was 10-15 mg/l whereas in the agricultural zones south of Brussels the figure rises to 20-50 mg/l and in the lowland and coastal areas of intensive agriculture with cattle and pig breeding the figure rises to 100mg/l during the winter months. In Germany, the main areas affected by high readings were areas of intensive agriculture or special cultivation (such as viniculture) or where pasture land had been ploughed up. In Italy, pollution of underground water sources was widespread in all areas of intensive agricultural activity and in the United Kingdom the highest concentrations were in areas of low rainfall and more intensive agriculture like central and southern England.

Against this background, there have been increasing pressures from Brussels for tighter controls on agricultural activity to protect the quality of water. The preamble to Council Directive 91/676 of 12 December 1991 states:

> *By encouraging good agricultural practices, member states can provide all waters with a general level of protection against pollution in the future.*

Traditionally ground water has been a cheap source of water supply and the quality in the United Kingdom has been good. However, an increase in nitrate and organic compounds to ground water could lead to a substantial increase in the cost of making ground water suitable for human consumption. Several European countries, particularly Denmark and Holland, have laws which impose stricter controls on agricultural activities than the United Kingdom. Should these greater restrictions be introduced to the United Kingdom?

There are two main targets for legislative change. The first is the reduction in livestock levels and controls over the disposal of animal waste. The second is the reduction in the area of land under production or the reduction in the level of land use, associated with a reduction in agricultural chemical input.

Many members of the European Union have a compulsory control on livestock density and on the disposal of farm waste. In Belgium, for example, animals are limited to four adult cattle equivalent per hectare; permission is required for the storage of slurry within a radius of two kilometres of ground water collection points, new animal housing must contain six months manure storage capacity. and there is a limit on the size of indoor livestock units which have no outdoor grazing facilities.

In 1988 Council Directive 88/708 introduced measures to lay down the maximum quantity of animal manures that could be applied to land and introduced rules covering methods of application and storage capacity. These rules echo the sort of restriction imposed in Belgium. The detailed implementation of the Directive was left to member states. To the extent proposals went beyond the requirements of good agricultural practice, the Commission allowed member states to include appropriate technical and/or financial assistance to help farmers adapt to the new agro-economic context.

In the United Kingdom, there followed a debate over whether compulsory controls were the best approach. It is declared government policy to avoid regulation wherever possible and to achieve their environmental objectives by non-regulatory means (see the MAFF consultation document on Environmental Schemes under the Common Agricultural Policy May 1993). This view was supported by the former National Rivers Authority.

In its publication Water Quality Series Number 6, January 1992, the National Rivers Authority (NRA) expressed the view that the introduction of compulsory controls on the number of animals per hectare, storage capacity and the disposal of animal wastes on land was not required and that a more structured voluntary approach would suffice.

The NRA had two main proposals. The first was that the relevant authorities should assist commercial organisations in the research and development of effective treatment systems for farm waste and that MAFF encourage their introduction by grant aid procedures. The second proposal was that individual farm waste management plans should be prepared to assist farmers how best to cope with their waste and that such management plans should be grant aided to encourage rapid uptake. The NRA believed that the extent to which the process of spreading agricultural waste on land was successful in avoiding pollution was dependent primarily on local management. It was convinced that farmers generally know their land well and that some technical guidance could develop simple practical waste management plans which would ensure sound disposal regimes for all waste on land or elsewhere.

The approach of the NRA was not echoed by the Royal Commission on Environmental Pollution in its 16th report dated June 1992. The Commission expressed the view that such measures were not sufficient to reduce to acceptable levels the risk of serious water pollution. Livestock units which do not have access to sufficient land suitable for safe disposal should be required to provide or arrange treatment for excess animal wastes. In addition, the Commission recommended that operators of intensive livestock units above a specified size should be subject to an authorization system to be operated by the agricultural departments.

Regulations have been introduced in a number of areas in recent years. For example, the European Council Directive 91/676 of 12 December 1991 imposed a duty on member states to designate Nitrate Vulnerable Zones and to establish action programmes in respect of those zones comprising the mandatory measures specified in Annex III to the Directive.

Annex III required that the action programme should include rules relating to the capacity of storage vessels for livestock manure and rules to ensure that for each farm or livestock unit the amount of livestock manure applied to the land each year should not exceed a specified amount per hectare. In order to assess the effectiveness of these zones, the Directive required the monitoring of the nitrate concentration in fresh waters over a period of one year.

The initial response of the former National Rivers Authority to Directive 91/676 was luke warm. In Water Quality Series Report Number 6, January 1992, the NRA stated:

Vulnerable zones will occupy much of the land area of England and Wales and, for ground waters, there will be too many to designate within the two year period allowed. Furthermore, continued use of storage and blending by the water companies is likely to enable the majority of problems to be overcome within the foreseeable future.

Nevertheless, the NRA did produce a groundwater protection policy. It announced general measures to protect aquifers as well as plans for specific Groundwater Protection Zones around water supplies and a groundwater vulnerable mapping programme. Groundwater vulnerability maps advise on the susceptibility of groundwaters to pollution. The intention was that such maps would be used to help planners and the NRA decide on the siting of operations which have the potential to pollute groundwaters.

These regulations have been linked with an increase in the controls through the planning system on agricultural activities. Although Section 55 of the Town and Country Planning Act 1990 provides that the use of any land for the purposes of agriculture or forestry or any building occupied with such land does not constitute development for which planning permission is required, there are special controls over the location of intensive livestock units and sludge and slurry operations within 400 metres of a protected building (which includes houses) and, with effect from the 2 January 1992 under the Town and Country Planning General Development (Amendment) (Number 3) Order 1991, local planning authorities must received prior notification in respect of the siting, design and external appearance of buildings on agricultural land.

The second target for legislative change - a reduction in the area of land under production and the reduction in the level of land use, associated with a reduction in agricultural chemical input - has seen increased legal controls in recent years also.

Prior to 1988 there were virtually no legal controls on these matters anywhere in Europe. France had laws which tried to ensure that only the correct amount of nitrogen was applied to crops and that fertiliser was applied at the correct time of year. Germany had similar laws which referred to the "normal amount with regard to the fertilisation of agricultural land" and made the link between the application of liquid manure, chemical fertiliser and animal manures. Denmark introduced a law in 1987 on chemical fertilisers which required all farmers to establish vegetation on the land in the months up to October 20th to try and reduce nitrate leaching from the soil. The area covered by the scheme was expanded from 45% in 1988 to 55% in 1989 and 65% in 1990. Only Belgium had laws which placed specific limits on the amount of fertiliser which could be applied to land - 440kgn per hectare. Greece, Ireland, the Netherlands, Portugal and Spain had no regulation at all on the use of chemical fertilisers.

In 1988 the European Community introduced the Set Aside scheme by Council Regulation 1094/88. The implementation of the regulation in the United Kingdom was provided by Statutory Instrument SI 1988 number 1352 (as subsequently amended). This scheme was designed to take land out of agricultural production and imposed conditions on the farming regime in set aside areas.

In the same year the European Council proposed the establishment of rules for the application of chemical fertiliser specifying maximum levels of application, periods during which application was prohibited and indicating a minimum distance from a water course for application. Records were to be kept of the total quantities of nitrate applied to land. The details are contained in the annex to Council Directive 91/676 dated 12 December 1991.

The initial set aside regulations failed to have a significant impact on arable production. This was primarily because the level of payments for set aside land resulted in farmers participating in the scheme only in relation to their marginal low quality land. According to Hawke Robinson and Kovleva in their article "Set Aside its legal framework and environmental protection" no more than 0.7% of UK agricultural land was involved in the set aside programme.

The shortcomings of the set aside regime led to the introduction of new regulations agreed by the European Council of Ministers on 21 May 1992. These were implemented in June 1992 as Council Regulations 2078/92, 2079/92 and 2080/92. The main feature of the new scheme was the introduction of measures designed to have a beneficial impact on the environment. A prime element was the introduction of non-rotational set aside which permitted farmers to leave the same land set aside year after year. The set aside scheme is associated with a number of other schemes (such as the Meadowland Scheme and the Habitat Improvement Scheme) designed to provide environmental enhancement.

The new set aside scheme was accompanied with new management rules which were announced on 28 July 1993 for the period 1993/94. These management rules contained detailed cropping requirements.

Figures produced by the Ministry of Agriculture Fisheries and Food show that the quantity of fertiliser and pesticide use in agriculture in the United Kingdom has reduced in recent years. However, this situation is attributable to a number of reasons not associated with legal controls.

There has been an improved understanding of the operation of nitrogen on crops and the impact of different cropping methods on nitrogen dispersion. As a result, farmers have reduced Autumn nitrogen applications to winter cereals from about 60% of the area in 1985 to under 20% of the area in 1989. Nitrogen application rates on grassland have declined and nitrogen usage on sugar beet has declined following research which indicates that excessive use of nitrogen depresses sugar yields.

Plant breeding techniques and biological control systems have improved. Whilst there are still tight controls on genetically modified organisms and the Department of the Environment does not anticipate extensive use of such organisms until the turn of the century, such developments do reduce the need for conventional use of fertilisers and pesticides.

Increased mechanisation has improved the efficiency and timeliness of cultivations to facilitate higher yields without chemical applications. Net farm incomes in real terms for arable farms (most likely to use fertiliser and pesticide) declined during the 1980s. As a result, the level of expenditure on chemical use has declined particularly since recent evidence such as the article by D Richardson in the *Financial Times* on 4 February 1992 showed that between 10% and 60% of fertiliser may not be taken up by crops.

The announcement by the UK government in October 1995 of the creation of a Pesticide Forum to encourage the adoption of pesticide minimisation techniques and promote their uptake through training and guidance appears to demonstrate that the UK government recognises the significance of education rather than legal controls in this area.

The European Union itself appears to question whether its policies of increasing regulation have led to an improvement in water quality. The report of the European Commission entitled The State of the Environment in the European Community (which accompanied the Commission's proposals to the European Council for the adoption of a community programme of policy and action in relation to the environment - the fifth action programme) states that generally the state of the community water resources has not improved. There are far more examples of deterioration in quality than in improvements. The report points to an increasing deterioration in ground water quality and damaged coastal waters and estuaries by pollution or eutrophication and increasing demand on resources. It calls for further vigorous action both on point source and non-point source pollution.

Experience outside the European Union suggests that simply to increase the level of regulation is not the solution to an improvement in water quality. In Canada, the key to Ontario's non-point source pollution strategy is the 1978 Great Lakes Water Quality Agreement between the United States of America and Canada. This policy is based on one of research, education and incentive programmes designed to modify management practices rather than that of a strict regulatory policy. The approach appears to be working. According to Michael Jeffery QC at the IBA Conference in San Francisco in June 1992 the grant and incentive system with its emphasis on education has engendered co-operation within the agricultural community which has translated into efforts to meet and surpass goals aimed at changing traditional practices to more environmentally sound ones. Control of non-point source pollution poses a difficult

31

challenge to regulators because even simple identification is problematic.

There appears to be no comprehensive study which has attempted analysis of the impact of legal controls on agricultural activity as a means of improving water quality on the basis of an assessment of the costs, the benefits and the risks. The nearest attempt is the study by the Department of the Environment of the economic and other consequences of the various local options limiting nitrate concentrations in drinking water (the Nitrate Issue, December 1988).

The main conclusion reached by the study was that due to the wide variability of water catchment size, hydrogeology, climatic conditions, land use and availability of alternative water sources any solution would need to take into account local circumstances and the special characteristics of each area. The study highlighted also the contrasting conclusions which could be drawn depending on whether the approach used was based on local cost or national resource implication. The general conclusion of the study was that the impact of agricultural pollution on water resources is not best solved by restrictions on agricultural activity alone and indeed is not capable of solution in practice by such means alone either.

The study looked particularly at the different characteristics of areas based on soil type, distinguishing between chalk areas, limestone and sandstone to see whether enforced changes in the pattern of agricultural activity would be effective in reducing the nitrate concentration in drinking water to the target standard of 45 mg/l. The desk studies concluded:

1. The ground water in all three chalk areas examined would respond only extremely slowly to changes in agricultural practice. Even if the entire catchment area was put down to non-fertilised grass now, the intended reduction in ground water nitrate concentration to 45 mg/l would not be achieved by the year 2040.

2. In one limestone area examined, the target reduction could be achieved by minimal farming changes, assuming no intensification of the existing relatively extensive pattern of farming there.

3. In another limestone catchment area the option of blending high and low nitrate waters was cheaper than requiring farming changes but the availability of an alternative water source was a major factor.

4. In 3 of the 4 sandstone areas examined, the water treatment/blending/replacement option was much cheaper in every case than the option of requiring changes in agricultural practice if measured on a local cost basis, although on a national resource analysis the agricultural options were cheaper.

5. In four areas where an agricultural practice change was assessed to be the least cost option on a national resource basis, this option would not itself achieve the imposed target within the relevant time scale.

The best solution appeared to be, therefore, a combination of some changes in agricultural activity and action by the water companies in water treatment blending and replacement (including the use of aquifer recharge schemes and phosphorous stripping techniques). Prevention of pollution by restrictions on activities must be linked with enhanced methods of water treatment. The Hatton Catchment Nitrate Study of the Hatton Area of Staffordshire produced by Severn-Trent Water demonstrated that a combination of prevention methods (the reduction of the amount of nitrate leached into the aquifer) and cure methods (treatment or blending water after it has been abstracted or by source replacement) produces a more cost effective result than using "prevention" or "cure" options on their own.

The NRA Water Quality Series Report Number 6, 1992, whilst supporting the view that the disposal of a range of agricultural waste and by-products to land is the soundest option, makes it quite clear that the extent to which this process is successful in avoiding pollution is dependent on many factors - with local management being the overriding one. In short, if a policy is to be effective then it must be backed up by a system of education to ensure that those involved in the agricultural industry are aware of the cause of the problems and the technical basis and means for their solution.

A recent study by the Ministry of Agriculture (MAFF) reported in the ENDS report May 1996 suggests that further education is necessary on many British farms. MAFF commissioned market research to assess awareness and effectiveness of the codes of good agricultural practice which were published between 1991 and 1993 and farmers' attitudes to them. More than half of farmers questioned were not even aware of official codes of practice on environmental protection. MAFF's advice on issues like soil protection were not reaching most farmers, almost 40% of whom were not complying with good agricultural practice.

A difference was found between the performance of farmers having copies of the codes of practice from those who did not. Whilst more than 38% did not comply with good agricultural practice, those who had copies of the codes performed better than average. 52% of farmers were described as "pollution friendly", 23% as "neutral" and 26% as "pollution unfriendly". Farmers known to have copies of the various codes performed better with 81% in the "pollution friendly" class and 11% in the "neutral" class.

The poorest areas of compliance for arable farmers were containing pesticide spillages (38%) correct disposal of pesticide containers (14%) and avoiding soil erosion (25%). The best compliance was matching fertiliser applications to crop needs (62%) and avoiding soil compaction (57%). Whilst the code of good agricultural practice for the protection of water was the most widely known code amongst farmers, only 18% of farmers were found to have the code.

Nine out of ten farmers agreed that the prevention of water pollution through the safe handling of pesticides, slurry and silage was important. However, very few farmers were open to the idea that they needed more advice. The survey concludes that, whilst farmers with codes have often taken action as a result, many are reluctant to make pro-active management changes for the sake of more environment-friendly farming. The researchers found that the promotion and enforcement of the codes was lacking and recommended that measures be taken to disseminate the codes more widely. Clearly there is plenty of scope for more education in this area.

Before any further consideration is given to any further regulation of agricultural activity in order to improve water quality there are a number of issues which need to be addressed. Specific areas for consideration include:

1. The basic concern expressed by many commentators is that the move towards further legislation is based on inadequate research. The realisation of the problems created by nitrate, particularly in ground water, in relatively recent times, associated with the slow movement of pollution of ground water has meant that the link between cause and effect has been difficult to prove statistically. The Department of the Environment report "Assessment of Ground Water Quality in England and Wales" (1988) states:

   Much has been achieved in understanding nitrate movement in aquifers although there are still gaps in knowledge in the soil or shallow unsaturated zones.

Further research is necessary to establish whether the statutory maximum admissible concentration of nitrate in drinking water at 50mg/l of nitrate is the correct standard. This standard is based on the European Community Directive 80/68 which was based itself on the standard set by the World Health Organisation in 1970 to protect infants from Blue Baby Syndrome. However, the WHO stated that a supply in the range of 50 to 100mg/l was acceptable provided community physicians in the area concerned were warned to look out for the possible occurrence of Blue Baby Syndrome. The Royal Commission on Environmental Pollution in its 16th report on Freshwater Quality (1992) states:

We have not been convinced that this strict limit (50mg per litre of nitrate) is needed to safeguard health in the UK or any other country with a satisfactory public water supply system. We regret that the EC limit has created anxiety in the minds of consumers whose supplies are known to be marginally in breach of the limit, has removed from use several water sources which were regarded as secure, possibly diverted resources and attention from more deserving objectives and created some environmental problems in disposing of nitrate removed from supplies.

As long ago as 1985, the Government's chief medical officer stated that there had been no reported cases of Blue Baby syndrome since 1972 and only 14 since 1945. Until further research has established the safe level of nitrate in the water, further regulation would be premature.

It is necessary to find a method of funding the research. The former National Rivers Authority recommended that the government did this by two methods. The first was the use of taxation. The second was the extension of the manufacturers levy on chemicals. The wisdom of this policy has been doubted by the Royal Commission on Environmental Pollution in its 16th report. It has stated that demand for both pesticides and artificial fertilisers seem relatively insensitive to their price. However, the use of a levy would be consistent with the "polluter pays" principle.

2.   The dispute over the impact of phosphorous input from agriculture on the eutrophication of UK waters needs to be resolved. Following a report in 1990 by Professor Brian Moss, the government claimed that eutrophication problems were restricted to a few localised sites in the United Kingdom. Professor Moss has declared subsequently that his report was misquoted for political ends. A recent report by the Department of Agriculture for Northern Ireland suggests that many water bodies in the UK are under threat. A study of Lough Neagh (one of the lakes studied in Professor Moss' original report) shows an increase in the phosphorous concentration since 1988 despite the fact that phosphorous has been stripped progressively from sewage discharges to the Lough - suggesting that the increase is coming from diffuse agricultural sources. The DANI report suggests that it is likely that increasing phosphorous levels in soils are threatening lakes in northern and western Britain as well which have similar agricultural systems. Despite this, the government's report on sustainable development indicators published in March 1996 asserts that:

The majority of UK waters are free from eutrophication.

A eutrophication strategy is to be launched shortly by the Environment Agency. This will include analysis to establish historic and current nutrient levels in waters on a catchment by catchment basis. Until then, the Agency will not have an overview of the situation. This is another example where inadequate research and understanding of the scientific position needs remedying before any further controls are implemented.

3.   Any approach to improvement of water quality must be based on an assessment of the cost and the benefit of the approach adopted. The Parliamentary Office of Science and Technology produced a report in May 1993 on its investigations into whether a cost benefit analysis would yield the same standards and priorities for expenditure on water treatment as are required by the European Community Directive on drinking water standards (Directive 80/778).

It commented that safety standards always involve a trade off between costs and benefits (otherwise regulatory bodies would set zero standards for all contaminants) and cost benefit methods can be seen as a way of rationalising this process. It referred to the need for the European Union to pay more attention to the balance of costs and benefits in its proposal. It concluded that if the European Union maximum admissible concentrations of nitrates, lead and pesticides were reviewed on the basis of a quantitative risk assessment, the justification on scientific and cost benefit grounds for the current nitrate and pesticide standards could face substantial challenge. At the very least, the priority given by the current regulations to removing nitrates and pesticides is misplaced and a given expenditure would have much greater potential to benefit health if devoted to reducing exposure to lead.

This approach appears to have been accepted in the UK to some extent. When the former NRA announced its plans for statutory water quality objectives in January 1996 it was ordered by the Department of the Environment to prepare cost benefit assessments of its proposals before they were introduced.

4. Pure cost benefit analysis alone fails to address the issue of public perception of risk. Many customers of water companies do not want pesticides in drinking water irrespective of any scientific considerations regarding "safe" levels. The Parliamentary Office of Science and Technology in its report in May 1993 indicates that social scientists suggest that it is in the area of risk perception that the greatest progress is needed. There are numerous examples where the public view of the adequacy of proposed control measures is not related to the actual level of risk.

A recent House of Lords Committee Report on drinking water (4th Report Session 1995 - 1996 HMSO) looked at the present level of pesticides in drinking water. The British Agrochemicals Association gave evidence to the committee that the present limits were totally arbitrary, unscientific and out of date and might prevent the introduction of safer new pesticides or the re-registration of existing pesticides. The BAA claimed that a relaxation of the standard would not result in any increase in pesticide levels. The present limit for individual pesticides in drinking water is 0.1 UG/L. The European Commission proposes the retention of this limit. The British Government wants to replace it by separate standards based on the toxicology of individual pesticides. The House of Lords Committee supported the view of the European Commission. They stated that there were strong political reasons for maintaining the standard irrespective of public health considerations. Although not specified, strong political reasons may refer to public perception. Education of the public is critical, therefore, once adequate research has been done to establish the level of risk.

5. In the United Kingdom the focus for legislative changes has been concerned primarily with water quality and not water quantity. As a result of the reduction in industrial capacity the level of water consumption has not increased in the United Kingdom in the last decade. Whilst water quantity is not currently an issue in the United Kingdom in relation to agricultural activity, it should not be ignored. It appears that 90% of population growth in the next 50 years will be in urban areas which will necessarily mean that demand for water will increase. At the same time, if water quality standards continue to rise, there will be diminishing sources of water of adequate quality. This factor combined with a series of dry winters and hot summers could give rise to regular concern over the quantity of water available. This problem exists already in the United States. In Los Angeles, for example, the City authorities have negotiated a contract with a group of farmers. This involves the city providing funding to enable the farmers to reduce irrigation wastage in order to free up water for use in the City. Similar schemes may need to be introduced for farmers in the United Kingdom in the future. However, there is clearly a need also for education of the urban public about the need to reduce water consumption.

6. The existing system of legal controls suffers seriously from a lack of coherent approach. There is a lack of overall policy coherence, partly due to an evolving, sometimes shifting,

agenda on both the scope of policy and the nature of legislation. The administration of legislation has been divided between numerous bodies. Water Management policies need to be integrated within the wider environment framework as well as with other policies dealing with human activities such as agriculture, industry, energy, transport and tourism. A united approach is required to ground water protection and surface water protection. These problems are recognised by the announcement that a strategy for integrated planning and management of water resources is proposed by the European Commission.

7.   If education is to mean anything in this context, consideration should be given to removing strict liability from certain statutory offences. Under the Water Resources Act 1991 many of the offences are ones of "strict liability" requiring proof of the proscribed Act but no wilful or negligent intent. The only significant defence is that the offence was due to causes over which the person had no control. In Australia the defence of "due diligence" is available. This defence was analysed in the case of SPCC -v- Kelly (unreported Land and Environment Court 16 March 1992).

Due diligence... contemplates a mind concentrated on the likely risks. The requirements are not satisfied by precautions merely as a general matter in the business of the corporation, unless also designed to prevent the contravention.

Due diligence is in many respects the converse of negligence and evidence must be produced to exhibit a concerned state of mind and steps taken which seek to ensure that all reasonable effort was made to prevent the prohibited action. In establishing a due diligence offence, it is necessary to prove the existence of the system (which is supervised) to prevent offences occurring and also to convince the Court (with the benefit of hindsight) that the system is reasonable in the circumstances to prevent all foreseeable risks. Whilst strict liability may be seen as more likely to result in a conviction, there can be little incentive to introduce control systems to avoid pollution if the existence of those systems does not provide any defence to a prosecution.

Whatever technical criteria are employed to assess how legal controls on agricultural activities might lead to improvements in water quality the decision will be based to some extent on some criteria which are essentially political or philosophical. There may be a political preference for compulsory controls rather than voluntary regulation or vice versa. The present government policy is to avoid regulation unnecessarily and to make a cost compliance assessment of its proposals on business. Such political priorities may change.

There may be political pressure to take action before there is statistical evidence to support the assumptions on which proposed policy changes are based. The protection of the environment or the maintenance of the rural economy may be perceived as more important factors than costs. Environmental groups emphasise the importance of the maintenance of species diversity and amenities.

The pressure from Europe for increased legal controls on agricultural activity in order to improve water quality is not the correct approach. It is clearly sensible to use the opportunity of agricultural overproduction to promote schemes for environmental protection which will have a beneficial effect on water quality. There are ways in which the current legal framework can be streamlined. Nevertheless, the case for wholesale increase in restrictions is not made and controls on agricultural activities alone will not provide an improvement in water quality.

More important is improvement of local management by farmers through education. Further research is necessary into safe levels of pollutant in the water and education of the public in the perception of risk. There are serious concerns about the quality standards on which some proposals for further restrictions are based. There is a clear need for further research and monitoring to provide statistical information on which to make an informed judgement and a programme of education. This approach involves an element of risk because a delay may result in irreparable damage to the water environment, particularly ground water. However, on the evidence currently available the costs involved in the imposition of greater restrictions do not appear to be justified by the quantifiable risks.

4 Implementation of the Environmental Impact Assessment Process in Sri Lanka - The Story of the Defeat of a Hydroelectric Dam Project

William W Westerfield, III
Senior Visiting Fellow, Law Faculty, Southampton Institute

Hemantha Withanage
Senior Environmental Scientist, Environmental Foundation, Ltd.

Introduction

This paper will examine the story of the defeat of the Upper Kotmale Hydro-Project ("UKHP"), an ill-conceived hydroelectric dam project in the Central Highlands of Sri Lanka. Quite simply, the project was defeated because its sponsors failed to convince the relevant government authorities that they had chosen the least environmentally damaging alternative for development, as required by Sri Lanka's environmental impact assessment ("EIA") law. The real story, however, is about the success of the environmental impact assessment process in a developing country in Asia. In this instance, at least, the law worked as it was intended - that is, it allowed groups of concerned citizens to force a public review of the adverse environmental impacts of a major development. The review subsequently led to the project's disapproval.

However this outcome was not achieved easily. It required a rapid and highly organized response from the environmental community. The response had two basic goals: (1) to make a technical and legal case against the UKHP according to the formal procedures of Sri Lanka's EIA law; and (2) to rally public opinion against the dam project in order to put pressure on the government to follow the law. The environmental community in Sri Lanka succeeded brilliantly on both fronts. But it was only through intelligent planning and execution, completed with a great deal of hard work, that these goals were attained.

This paper will focus on how these goals were actually accomplished. In order to explain the strategy and tactics used by the opponents of the UKHP it will be necessary to describe Sri Lanka's EIA process in substantial detail. At the risk of distracting the casual reader, this in discussion is also intended to give the legal practitioner an accurate guide as to how Sri Lanka's EIA law is supposed to work.

Following this foundation, attention will turn to the UKHP and how the environmental community in Sri Lanka organized the campaign against it. The concern here will be to show the likely problems to be encountered by the public when using the EIA process in their own countries (assuming that the legal procedures are generally similar), and to illustrate how these pitfalls can be overcome. Of particular interest to this discussion is the process of environmental education in mobilizing essentially ignorant local villagers to speak up on development projects that affect them.

Finally, the paper will conclude with a number of suggested improvements to the EIA process in developing countries. It is hoped that a discussion of these aspects of the EIA process will bridge the gap between academic treatments of how the EIA process should work on paper, and how it can be made to work in practice. However, to begin with, it would be useful to provide some background on how recent development in Sri Lanka has given rise to its EIA law.

A. Sri Lanka's Development Pains

Once renowned for its thick tropical forests, gems and spices, ancient travellers referred to Sri Lanka as the "pearl of the Indian Ocean". However, Sri Lanka is changing rapidly. In the early 1990s, the Sri Lankan economy grew by 9% in real terms, led by a powerful expansion of private sector manufacturing. Though the resumption of hostilities with the Liberation Tigers of Tamil Eelam (popularly known as the Tamil Tigers) has slowed the annual growth rate to the range of 5 to 5.5%, the long term outlook remains bright.[1]

In addition to capital, land and labour, an industrialized society must have electricity to drive its economy. By the mid-1980s, the demand for electricity in Sri Lanka was rising by 10% per year, a growth rate which has continued in recent years.[2]

But Sri Lanka has no fossil fuels to meet the burgeoning demand. Instead, seasonal rainfall over the Hill Country creates its only indigenous energy source -- hydroelectric power. Accordingly, Sri Lanka's national utility, the Ceylon Electricity Board, made the decision in the early 1980s to eschew power generation by costly imports of fossil fuels, and to develop its hydroelectric potential. As of September 1995, Sri Lanka had a total generating capacity of about 1,400 MW of electricity, of which 1,135 MW (or 81%) was being generated by 15 hydrostations.[3]

Though hydro-electric power generation is a relatively cheap and clean source of energy, it is not without its environmental costs. Dam projects affect larger areas of terrain than any other type of power generation. Unlike a large factory or even a fossil fuel-fired power station, dams can divert watercourses and, in effect, erase hundreds of hectares of land from the landscape. Moreover, large hydro-electric dam projects can exacerbate a host of other problems - loss of forest cover, extensive agricultural expansion on erosive land, land salinization, loss of ancient tank systems, and loss of habitat. Sri Lanka has suffered particularly hard from these environmental consequences of its drive for industrialization. The most profound has been the loss of almost half of its remaining tropical rain forests in only 40 years. It is estimated that in 1956, for example, forest covered 44% of its land area.

By 1992, that figure had been reduced to only 24%.[4] Among the most frequently cited reasons for this rapid deforestation are ill-planned, large-scale development projects,[5] though illicit cutting of trees for fuelwood and timber, and forest clearing for cultivation are also cited.[6]

The Mahaweli River project is a prime example. This massive undertaking was designed to divert water from the wet southwest region of the country to develop the dry southeast quadrant. As of 1992, the project affected 364,372 hectares of land and cost over US $10.4 billions in grants and loans.[7] While bringing needed power, welcome income and opportunities, a recent internal World Bank study admits that the environmental impact of the scheme has been devastating.[8] Yet another example is the gigantic US $440 million Samanalawewa hydroelectric project in Sabaragamuwa Province, Sri Lanka. Planned without adequate environmental impact assessment, this project has had wide-ranging environmental and social impacts, from the loss of rare forests and fish to the displacement of local farmers. The failure to conduct a proper EIA also led to expensive hydrogeologic remediation because water from the dam's reservoir leaked into old quarries.[9]

One relatively unique impact of Sri Lanka's large dam projects has been the loss of waterfalls. Originally, Sri Lanka had 18 major waterfalls, but hydroelectric dams caused the destruction of three important waterfalls -- the Laksapana and Aberdeen Falls in 1953, and Victoria Falls in 1980.[10]

The decline in forest cover caused by the Mahaweli River project and development projects in other catchment areas has also had the unintended consequence of actually *reducing* water supplies. With fewer trees in catchment areas to absorb water during the rainy season, important springs lose their flow during the dry period. This phenomenon and recently unfavourable weather conditions has led to a serious water shortage for Mahaweli power stations, which in turn has caused daily power cuts of between six to eight hours from April to June 1996. Obviously, such serious power cuts not only inconvenience the public but also jeopardize development.

While past Sri Lanka governments have supported large development projects in order to supply needed power and infrastructure, in the early 1990s the government at last recognized that large-scale projects were threatening Sri Lanka's heritage -- those environmental and cultural treasures that make it unique. In 1992, for example, Stanley Kalpage, Sri Lanka's ambassador to the United Nations, declared that "the Sri Lankan government is very conscious of the country's ecological problems and plans to introduce stringent laws to restrict pollution, save forests, prevent soil erosion, protect the ozone layer and arrest environmental degradation."[11] One of the principal remedies employed by the government to carry out its pledge was the adoption of a western-style EIA law in 1981. According to Mr. Kalpage, all industrial and development projects in Sri Lanka would first be subjected to an EIA, and that "[a]ny project that fails to make the grade will not be approved by the government."[12]

But passing a law is only one step along the bumpy road of change. Implementing the law is what matters, and implementation has many obstacles. The Sri Lankan government, like governments everywhere, contain competing interests which support and oppose developments in relation to their bureaucratic goals. Thus, despite all the good laws and policies, there are powerful forces within government that press for their favourite projects, and see even profound environmental impacts as simply the price of progress. As will be seen below, these forces were at work in support of the UKHP despite all of its obvious environmental problems.

B. The Environmental Impact Assessment Process in Sri Lanka

The EIA process took hold in Sri Lanka rather slowly. The concept was first introduced in the 1981 Coastal Conservation Act, but was never implemented or enforced.[13]

Pressure for a comprehensive and functional EIA process built during Sri Lanka's attempts to draft a forestry master plan in the mid-1980s. Originally funded with the assistance of Finnida (the Finnish aid agency), Finnida withdrew support in response to the public outcry over the government's failure to allow public input to the plan.[14] When the World Bank stepped in to finish the plan, its version, also drafted without public input, was criticized for failing to curb deforestation by organized parties, often with direct support from political elements, while preventing traditional communities from extracting timber for fuelwood and other subsistence purposes.[15] This criticism forced the World Bank to revise the plan and subject it to an EIA procedure and public debate. The result was to allow public participation in the actual management of tens of thousands of hectares of forests.[16] The development of the forestry master plan led the government to declare, "The state alone or the Forest Department alone cannot protect and manage the forests effectively without the participation of the local peoples, NGOs [non-governmental organizations] and the private sector."[17] This experience contributed to EIA requirements for projects throughout the country in the 1988 amendments to the National Environment Act (NEA).[18] The new rules were modelled after the American National Environmental Policy Act of 1969 ("NEPA"), which the government has described as "identical in concept, context and effect" to the NEA.[19] A key feature of NEPA is the requirement to assess alternatives to the proposed development.

The requirement to assess alternatives is also central to the EIA process in Sri Lanka. According to Mr. Cecil Amerasinghe, current Secretary to the Ministry of Transport, Environment and Women's Affairs (the "Environment Secretary"):

> I cannot over emphasize that an adequate and a rigorous consideration of alternatives is at the heart of the EIA decision-making process. It's through such a rigorous consideration of alternatives that are environmentally more friendly that decision makers, Project Proponents and the public can reach a conclusion on the sustainable way in which development projects can be evolved. The consideration of alternatives cannot be taken lightly nor reduced to a superficiality. What's required is an honest and rigorous consideration of feasible and reasonable alternatives that are environmentally better.[20]

Mr Amerasingh's statement illustrates that the intent of the EIA law in Sri Lanka is to provide decision makers, *and the public*, with a range of development alternatives in order to minimize adverse impacts of any proposed project on the environment.

Actual implementation of the EIA provisions of the NEA, however, had to await promulgation of regulations in 1993 (hereinafter "EIA regulations").[21] Sri Lanka's EIA regulations cover virtually all projects involving the development of forests, mines, rivers, fisheries, transportation, housing, hotels, waste disposal, and industry (hereinafter "prescribed projects").[22] The broad scope of the EIA regulations takes on particular importance because Sri Lanka has no body of developed planning law. The principal omission from the list of prescribed projects is for master plans. Thus, even though the government eventually conducted a strategic EIA for the forestry master plan described above, that procedure is not mandated under the EIA regulations and has not been followed since.[23]

Apart from the area of strategic planning, Sri Lanka's EIA regulations are actually quite progressive, even by Western standards.[24] But as in so many developing countries, Sri Lanka lags behind the West in the capacity of its government officials and citizens to use the procedures forged in open, western-style democracies. But as we shall see below, these shortcomings can be overcome by public interest groups which mobilize the public and make well-reasoned comments in the EIA process.

The process works as follows. Before a prescribed project may be built, the developer (or "project proponent") must obtain approval from the appropriate "project approving agency" (or "PAA"). The PAA is the government agency with principal authority over the project. The work of the PAA is overseen and coordinated by the Central Environmental Authority (the "CEA"), the agency charged with implementing the EIA regulations generally. The CEA has varied and real authority. The most important of its powers is the requirement that it concur in any major project approved by the PAA.[25]

The project proponent initiates the approval process by submitting preliminary information to the PAA for "scoping" -- that is, to allow the PAA to determine the scope of issues to consider in approving or disapproving the proposed action. First, the PAA must determine whether the project proponent should prepare a relatively simple "initial environmental examination" ("IEE") report, or a more in-depth environmental impact assessment (EIA) report for projects with significant impacts. The PAA then sets the terms of reference ("TOR") for the IEE or EIA reports.[26] However, unlike the EIA process in many western countries, the EIA regulations in Sri Lanka allow for public participation (with PAA approval) in this early, scoping stage.[27]

The actual procedures for preparing IEE or EIA reports, and the required content, are specified in guidance issued by the CEA. Without going into detail, the IEE or EIA reports are required essentially to analyze both the environmental consequences of the proposed action, and any alternative actions which would minimize adverse effects, and explain why such alternatives were rejected.[28] Once the IEE or EIA report is prepared and submitted, the PAA checks the report against the TOR. If the PAA is not satisfied with the report, it can return it to the project proponent for revision. But once the report is accepted, the PAA publishes notices in the government gazette and other newspapers informing the public where the report can be viewed and invites written comments.[29] The public has 30 days in which to submit written comments. In addition to written comments, the NEA specifies that the PAA *may*, "where it considers appropriate in the public interest" set a public hearing where people can speak in support of their written comments. Though the PAA has discretion in calling a public hearing, CEA guidance encourages public hearings.[30] According to law, only those who submit written comments may participate in the public hearing, though in practice that restriction is difficult to uphold.[31] Following any hearing and the close of the public comment period, the PAA must send all comments to the project proponent within six days. However, the project proponent has no time limit in which to respond. Once responses are submitted, the PAA again has only six days in which to approve the project, with or without conditions, or reject the project and explain why. The PAA is required to consider the public comments, and responses to such comments by the project proponent.

Despite these procedures, there is relatively little guidance to the PAAs for actual decision-making on prescribed projects. Among the scant direction is Environment Secretary Amerasinghe's admonition that PAAs must make an honest and rigorous evaluation of the proposed action and possible alternatives. Accordingly, PAAs have substantial discretion to decide whether to approve or disapprove projects, subject of course to the oversight of the CEA.

Finally, in addition to the preferential periods of time afforded to project proponents to prepare the EIA report and responses to comments, project proponents also have a unilateral right of appeal from rejections of projects by the PAA or CEA.[32] The right of appeal is to the Environment Secretary, whose decision is final. The Secretary has complete discretion whether to approve, reject or modify the project. The only recourse to opponents of an approved project is to challenge the approval in a court action.

C. The Upper Kotmale Hydropower Project and its Impacts

The proposed site of the Upper Kotmale Hydro Project was at Talawakelle, on the wet, western slope of Sri Lanka's central mountain zone, about 160 km southeast of the capital of Colombo. The UKHP had its genesis in the huge Mahaweli River project which, as mentioned earlier, was meant to irrigate the dry southeastern region with water from the wet western region.[33] The master plan for the development of the Mahaweli and its tributaries identified several possible dam sites in the Upper Kotmale region, but did not recommend any in particular for development. It was only after the Japanese International Co-operation Agency ("JICA") conducted a feasibility study on behalf of the UKHP's proponent, the Ceylon Electricity Board ("CEB"), that the Talawakelle site was proposed. It is significant that JICA recommended it solely on technical and economic grounds, and not after consideration of environmental impacts.[34]

In 1994, the CEB performed a further engineering study and an EIA of the different sites examined and proposed by JICA. As a result, it formulated five possible development alternatives for the UKHP. The CEB chose the alternative of constructing a run of river type project[35] at Talawakelle. In a nutshell, the CEB proposed a complicated project, which would dam five streams[36] and dig 22 kilometers of tunnels to divert water from those streams to a reservoir. The project was to have a generating capacity of 150 megawatts.[37]

The CEB hired a consortium of Japanese companies, "CNEC", to perform the 1994 EIA mentioned above.[38] And despite the provision in the EIA regulations for public participation in scoping, none was allowed in this case.[39]

In addition to various economic and technical considerations, the EIA prepared by CNEC showed that constructing the UKHP at Talawakelle would cause considerable environmental impacts. Of principal importance were the impacts on certain waterfalls. The UKHP threatened to cut off or modify river flows to eight waterfalls, three of which are considered major falls.[40] Altering so many major waterfalls was a particularly sensitive issue since the project would have affected 3 of only 10 major falls accessible by road in the country.

Another major impact of the project was potential geological damage. The area had been identified previously as a high earth vibration region,[41] particularly prone to erosion and earth slips.[42] Studies have shown that the frequency of earth slips increased following the construction of other Mahaweli dams and reservoirs, requiring over 300 million rupees to be spent for the rehabilitation of affected land.[43] The tunnelling, new water flows and earth-slips also threatened the planned underground generator house and switch-yard for the UKHP, as well as the tunnels themselves. Moreover, the CEB estimated that about 15% of the UKHP reservoir's capacity would be filled in annually,[44] necessitating frequent dredging.

From a human standpoint, there was the additional impact on local, primarily Tamil, villagers. The Talawakelle alternative would cause 432 families to be relocated with no permanent new settlement area identified. The reduced flow in the Kotmale River and tributaries would also reduce the amount of water available for commercial tea and private purposes to the remaining villagers. Also, past experience with Sri Lanka's other major irrigation schemes has shown that drying of river channels leads to an increase in malaria.[45]

Additionally, the UKHP would have destroyed the habitats of two rare and threatened species of reptiles and two rare and threatened amphibian species. The project also would have reduced the habitat of a rare species of fish and several rare orchids. In all, the UKHP caused numerous environmental and social impacts that weighed heavily against the expected 5% natural increase in generating capacity from the dam.

Despite these consequences, the CEB strongly promoted the UKHP at the Talawakelle site. In its EIA report, the CEB rejected other development alternatives as either uneconomic or environmentally adverse and asserted that the Talawakelle site was the "optimum development plan in light of careful examination in aspects of environment, economical and system analysis."[46] However, a statement by the technical evaluation committee ("TEC") appointed to advise the PAA on whether to approve the project belied this assertion. The TEC concluded that the CEB selected Talawakelle "purely on economic benefit cost analysis based on power generation benefits and construction costs."[47] The CEB also seems to have favoured the Talawakelle option because its Japanese financing was tied to that alternative.[48]

D. The Campaign Against the UKHP

These criticisms (and others) levelled by the PAA's own technical evaluation committee only emerged on appeal of the final rejection of the UKHP. That might never have taken place had it not been for a coordinated opposition campaign by a number of Sri Lanka's environmental NGOs. The leading NGO of the campaign against the UKHP was the Environmental Foundation Limited ("EFL"), Sri Lanka's oldest environmental NGO.[49]

Despite its small size (with only two scientists and two lawyers), the EFL has had a large impact on the EIA process in only a short time. In only three years since the EIA regulations came into effect, the EFL has submitted comments for most of the 40 IEEs and 25 EIAs conducted in the country. Probably its most noteworthy success was its opposition to the Colombo-Katunayaka Expressway, the first EIA performed under the 1993 EIA regulations. The EFL opposed that project because it would have necessitated relocating more than 2,000 families, disrupted water flows, caused flooding, and led to the loss of important wetlands. The EFL also defeated the Rajawela Golf and Hotel Project near the Victoria reservoir on similar grounds.[50]

In late 1994, anticipating the results of CNEC's EIA report, the EFL launched a three-pronged campaign -- technical, media and local. On the technical front, the EFL contacted other interested NGOs that could assist in an analysis of the technical issues of the project. Following publication of the EIA report, the EFL prepared detailed written comments on the project's impacts, and coordinated its comments with comments from other NGOs. This work required considerable scientific expertise, and led to the conclusions that the UKHP was geologically unsound and threatened numerous plant and animal species. The EFL understood that while public opposition had a serious role to play in drawing attention to the project, actual disapproval would depend upon technical considerations.

On the media front, the EFL launched a national publicity campaign. Once it had analyzed the environmental and social impacts, it gave the information in lay terms to sympathetic journalists. The EFL used national journalists that it had worked with over time, and as well as regional correspondents in the Talawakelle area. The EFL also organized a campaign of postcards and petitions to be sent to relevant government officers, politicians, and to Sri Lanka's president. Of particular importance in its publicity drive was the EFL's shrewd decision to employ a strategy of focusing on the most controversial aspect of the UKHP -- the impact of the UKHP on the waterfalls. It emphasized that other waterfalls had already been lost, making these even more precious to Sri Lanka's heritage.

Third, on the local front, the EFL encouraged villagers and students to launch a leaflet and poster campaign to make the public aware of the UKHP in the affected area. They used slogans such as:

- Do Not Destroy our Waterfalls;
- Save the Environment;
- Electricity is for Colombo, not for the villages;
- Energy for Colombo, environmental problems for us.

The EFL also sponsored more serious attempts to educate local people through seminars. Thus in conjunction with other NGOs,[51] the EFL led two seminars to educate villagers in the Talawakelle area on the impacts of the project and of their right to submit written comments and potentially oral comments at a public hearing.[52]

At the first seminar, the EFL found (not surprisingly) that the newspaper advertisements required under the EIA regulations had informed few members of the public of the proposed UKHP. Fewer people still had understood their right to comment on the project. Accordingly, during the first seminar, the EFL focused its efforts on how members of the public could obtain a copy of the EIA report and how to prepare and submit written comments. On the eve of the public hearing, the EFL organised a second seminar to prepare the villagers for the hearing. Again, the EFL found that many of the villagers attending the seminar were only vaguely aware of the proposed UKHP, and thus it had to concentrate much of its efforts at simply informing these people of the project and of its potential impacts.

The task of educating the villagers raised the difficult issue of just how unbiased the EFL should be in fulfilling the role of educator. The EFL took the view that its primary responsibility was as an unbiased educator rather than as an advocate against the project, even though it clearly opposed siting the UKHP at Talawakele. Nevertheless, the obvious impact of the project on the waterfalls and the realisation that the villagers would suffer the project's impacts without receiving the benefits was enough to stir their opposition. However educating the local villagers to the impacts of the project was not enough. The EFL and the other NGOs realized that in order for the villagers to act on their opposition to the UKHP the NGOs had to impress upon the villagers that they had the *right* to be heard. The idea of rights generally, and particularly of the right to participate in government decision-making, is an idea that can seem quite foreign to many people in developing countries. Moreover, even if this concept of rights is accepted, the mass of people are generally poor and because of historical roles generally lack the confidence to speak out. Thus, one of the most important tasks undertaken by the NGOs at its seminars was "raising the spirit" of the people to give them the confidence and knowledge to express their beliefs. As events at the public hearing subsequently demonstrated, this was done quite successfully.

The pubic hearing took place in Nuwara Eliya, the major hill country town near Talawakelle. About 100 people participated. Attending were the CEB, their consultants (CNEC), the PAA (the Ministry of Power and Energy), local officials, the press, NGOs, tea estate workers, and other members of the general public. Some groups appeared with signs and banners, and at times they erupted in chants and general noise-making.

Representatives of the NGOs who submitted written comments were the principal spokesmen in opposition to the project. The national NGOs generally emphasized the environmental impacts of loss of waterfalls, soil stability, sedimentation of the reservoir, and the effect on rare plants and animals. Local NGOs, naturally enough, concentrated on the villagers' concerns about the social impacts. The most often voiced concerns were:

- When we lose our land to the reservoir, where do we live?

- How much will we be paid for the loss of our land?

- You are asking us to sacrifice our land and villages for electricity for someone else. We have no electricity.

- Some people say that you can generate electricity in other ways, but no one can create waterfalls.

- What will happen to tourism if we lose our waterfalls?

- If we lose our water from the rivers, where will we get our drinking water and water for agriculture?

As it turned out, many villagers gave speeches in opposition to the project, and particularly effective were speeches given by local women. The voices in opposition to the plan far outnumbered those in support, which put the CEB heavily on the defensive. The sometimes raucous proceedings received substantial press coverage and the effect was quite damaging to the CEB's cause.

E. Rejection of the UKHP and Appeal

Within a week of the public hearing, the PAA's TEC rejected the project. The TEC concluded that (1) the waterfalls had been assigned no economic value in the CEB's cost-benefit analysis; (2) the environmental costs of the Talawakelle alternative could be "extremely high"; and (3) other development options were not adequately considered.[53]

Nevertheless, the Oversight Committee of the PAA decided to approve the project.[54] Though the CEB later acknowledged on appeal that the PAA must approve the project on *environmental*, as well as technical and economic grounds, the PAA simply urged the CEA to concur in approval based on "technical and economic" factors alone. Despite this, the CEA declined to do so. It agreed instead with the TEC, concluding that environmentally friendlier options had not been adequately considered and directed the CEB to develop such alternatives.

The CEB subsequently appealed to the Environment Secretary against the CEA's decision to reject the project, as provided for under the EIA regulations.

It was during this phase of the campaign that the EFL played another essential role in the defeat of the UKHP. During the appeal, the EFL again submitted written comments and argued in support of their comments at an oral hearing. The nature of the comments called for on appeal, however, were primarily legal, requiring a wholly different expertise and emphasis. In the end, the EFL prevailed and the Secretary upheld disapproval of the project.

In explaining his decision, the Secretary emphasized that the goal of Sri Lanka's EIA process is for the government decision-maker to approve the best technical, economic and environmental option. For that to take place, the project proponent had to demonstrate that all reasonable alternatives have received a "rigorous exploration and objective evaluation."[55] Furthermore in a quite progressive approach, the Secretary stated that in making the cost-benefit analyses of technical, financial and environmental factors, environmental assets (such as waterfalls), and social impacts (such as resettlement issues) should be "costed with available economic tools and methodologies, however insufficient or imperfect these may be."[56] The Secretary found the CEB's Talawakelle alternative wanting in these respects. The Secretary also found that the PAA has a duty to act in a quasi-judicial capacity, essentially requiring impartiality, and that its conduct in this case suggested bias that threatened to "erode confidence in the EIA process and system."[57]

F. Why the Campaign was Successful

There are many lessons to be learned from the campaign against the UKHP that extend well beyond the rules of law enunciated by Environment Secretary Amerasinghe. As an initial matter, an obvious limitation of the EIA process is that it can only operate in a relatively open society where honest and conscientious people occupy positions of power. Another fundamental lesson of the campaign against the UKHP is that success of the EIA process depends upon the existence of independent NGOs, which understand the EIA process and are capable of educating and organising the public. But after acknowledging these conditions, what specific lessons can be drawn to assist other groups to utilize the EIA process in their own communities?

First and foremost, the campaign succeeded because the EFL and other NGOs submitted compelling technical and legal arguments which convinced the CEA and later, the Environment Secretary that the Talawakelle alternative was not the best one. This was achieved in two ways. First, the EFL (and other NGOs) were ready to submit technical comments when the EIA report was published. Sri Lanka's EIA regulations, like many EIA laws around the world, allow only 30 days from date of publication of the EIA report in which to submit written comments. This leaves very little time to analyze scientific information to decide how to respond, especially where highly technical issues are involved. The only practical way of preparing comments in such a short time is by gathering most of the necessary information *before* the EIA report is even published and anticipating the comment period. In Sri Lanka, the EFL does this by monitoring upcoming projects throughout the country. One way is to look for public notices and to attend EIA scoping committee meetings wherever possible. Another, equally important method is to make effective use of personal contacts, both inside and outside the government. While in some cases this might lead to valuable "inside" information, more importantly it allows the NGO to keep abreast of events throughout the project approval process.

The second means by which the EFL were able to submit compelling written comments was by assembling technical expertise from a variety of sources. Scientific and technical analysis was obtained from at least four NGOs and coordinated so that the comments were mutually supportive. In this fashion, the EFL avoided the situation where technical experts on the same side of the issue espoused conflicting scientific views. Such unanimity was essential to garner sufficient credibility to counter the arguments of the CEB's professional consultants. This effort was only accomplished through diligent efforts to organise meetings of experts, to generate a coherent work product from those meetings, and to make coordinated oral presentations at the Nuwara Elyia hearing.

The other equally important goal of the opposition campaign was to stir public opinion against the UKHP in order to put public pressure on government officials to disapprove the project. At the very least, it was hoped that public attention would be drawn to the issue and thus would place public officials on notice that their decisions would be scrutinized. In this way, government decision-makers would be forced to act responsibly and in accordance with the law. This was accomplished through a variety of means.

The most obvious means was the effective use of publicity. The EFL drew national attention to the UKHP by engaging the national media and by sending postcards and petitions directly to national politicians. The EFL made this strategy more effective by concentrating on one issue -- the waterfalls. They did this because they realized that it is necessary to simplify issues in order to popularize them through the press. Similarly, the EFL drew local attention to the UKHP through newspapers, posters, leaflets, and the seminars. The goal of local publicity was to awaken the people to the project and its impacts with the hope that they would speak out at the public hearing. Again, the EFL's strategy of focusing on the waterfalls helped. However encouraging the local people to speak up was not simple task. First, the local villagers have to be made to care, or be reminded that they did care, about the waterfalls. To do this, the EFL employed a strategy of convincing the people that the threatened waterfalls were **their** waterfalls, and not some vague national possession. Additionally, the villagers had to be convinced or reminded that the waterfalls were worth saving - an amenity that must have seemed irrelevant to the daily lives of many. This was accomplished by appealing to people's higher values (such as aesthetics and pride) while simultaneously appealing to their practical concern that the waterfalls might damage earnings from existing and potential tourism. Indeed, the protests of the villagers at the public hearing showed that they understood these divergent concerns.

Nevertheless encouraging people to speak out involved more than awakening their concerns over losing waterfalls. The local villagers had to be encouraged and organized. The villagers of the Sri Lankan Hill Country, like rural people elsewhere in developing countries, do not have the tradition of challenging authority. Many have learned the hard way that doing so can bring retribution or even ruin. This attitude was perhaps stronger in this case because of the fact that the majority of villagers in the area were Tamils, a minority amidst the Singalese majority. Therefore, the EFL not only had to educate these people as to their rights in the EIA process, but also had to instill a sense of security that they could exercise those rights in safety. This was another, very important achievement of the seminars.

Underlying the tangible means of opposing the UKHP, good technical comments backed by public protest, were the intangible ingredients of success -- leadership, commitment, cooperation, and expertise. Of these qualities, perhaps the most important was the leadership of the EFL. The EFL developed the overall strategy and initiated the opposition. It organized the publicity campaign. It monitored the progress of the UKHP in the EIA process generally and the evolution of the CEB's EIA report in particular. It quickly organized consultations with scientists once the results of the EIA became known and then prepared technical comments based on those consultations. It drew in other NGOs. Without the EFL, there would have been no organized opposition. The importance of such leadership cannot be over emphasized.

Similarly, the campaign against the UKHP required sustained cooperation amongst the NGOs. Obviously, when groups work in concert the impact is more effective. This pattern was established when the NGOs prepared their written comments, and it culminated at the public hearing in Nuwara Elyia when the NGOs coordinated their oral comments so that each one concentrated on a different issue. This circumstance of presenting considered technical arguments against the backdrop of a boisterous chorus of the local villagers, allowed the opposition to speak, if not with a single voice, then in harmony.

Additionally, though the need for legal and technical expertise hardly needs elaborating, the impact of those skills on the local people merits comment. When an organisation such as the EFL gains a reputation for technical and particularly legal expertise, its prestige lends confidence to the public that their voices will be heard and that they are safe to speak in protest. This was another reason that the NGOs could rally public support.

Finally, credit should be paid to the design of Sri Lanka's EIA regulations. The National Environmental Act in Sri Lanka adopts a transparent and participatory approach that permits this kind of campaign. It also allows for public participation during scoping, which had it been allowed here might have avoided the ill-conceived Talawakelle option altogether. In any event, it makes public hearings easily available, which gives people a forum in which to present their views and to pressure the government to administer the EIA process properly. Public hearings are a vital safeguard of the EIA process everywhere, but they are especially important in developing countries where the traditions of public accountability, indeed honest government, are not long established.

While it is difficult to evaluate just how much influence the open process actually had on decision-makers in the case of the UKHP, it is one of the fundamental tenants of the EIA process that an open process, subject to public scrutiny, leads to better decision-making. Though the EIA process in Sri Lanka still suffers from numerous problems of implementation, (addressed next in the paper) the institutions of open government and a free press have combined to make the EIA process in Sri Lanka a viable one.

G. Problems and Suggested Remedies for Implementing the EIA Process in Developing Countries

While the defeat of the UKHP demonstrates that the EIA process **can** work in developing countries, it illustrates the problems to overcome in making it work. These problems include government bias towards development, abbreviated public comment periods, ignorance and a lack of democratic traditions of the mass of people, and a lack of commitment, training and a willingness to share power on the part of the educated elite. In all probability, these fundamental problems will continue to plague the process for the foreseeable future and there is little that committed advocates of EIAs can do about it, whether those advocates are as powerful as the World Bank, for example, or as marginal as a fledgling NGO. Nevertheless, a number of remedies should be considered for improving the implementation of the EIA process in developing countries.

1. The Legal Process

Problems with the EIA procedures in Sri Lanka are hardly unique to that country. Perhaps the biggest problem with the process is the short period of time available to the public to obtain the EIA report, and to prepare and submit comments. Under current EIA regulations, the public has only 30 days from the date notice is published in the government Gazette and selected newspapers informing them of where and when the IEE or EIA reports can be found. This very short period puts enormous pressure on NGOs, the public's leaders on these issues, and upon any individuals who wish to comment.

During the preparation of this paper, in February 1996, the Sri Lankan cabinet actually tried to increase the pressure by proposing to amend the NEA to *reduce* the public comment period from 30 days to only 14 days! This decision can only be seen as an effort by certain elements sympathetic to the industrial sector to discourage public participation in the EIA process. Nevertheless, as a result of effective lobbying by the EFL, the government agreed to keep the 30-day public comment period.

Rather than shorten the public comment period, the period should be lengthened to a more feasible period of time -- such as 60 or 90 days. As the matter now stands, developers have unlimited periods of time in which to prepare IEE and EIA reports. Salient facts within these reports are often difficult to understand (let alone verify) because the reports are typically written in technical language and often written to promote the project at issue. It is completely unreasonable to expect the public at large -- ignorant of the issues, unorganized and underfinanced -- to understand these reports and to prepare meaningful comments on technical issues in such a short period of time. At best, this role can be played by highly capable NGOs which are already established at the time the project comes up for approval. But such organizations do not always exist in the problem area, or have the capacity to deal with every development project which comes along. Only by lengthening the public comment period does the potential arise for individuals or newly formed groups to prepare informed comments. Since public participation is one of the fundamental goals of the EIA process, it should be facilitated by longer periods of time in which to prepare such comments.

In regard to the IEE/EIA reports themselves, a greater effort should be required of developers to make the reports available to the public. It is an unfortunate fact of life that publication of a notice of the availability of the IEE/EIA report in a newspaper (and particularly in a national gazette) is not enough to inform local people -- those most directly affected by development -- of their opportunity to comment. This practice of informing people through newspapers comes from western democracies, where traditions of universal literacy, a free press and protest are long-standing. These are not the traditions of many developing countries throughout the world. Publication of a single notice in a newspaper does not serve to inform traditional farmers and villagers. More should be done.

It would be an improvement to require developers to further notify the affected public through posters and leaflets, much as the EFL did when it organized local opposition to the UKHP. As the EFL demonstrated, this can be done quickly and inexpensively, which of course would serve the interests of developers by minimizing the delay in approving (or disapproving) projects. But the reality is that developers perceive that it is *not* in their interest to inform the public of their right to comment, as of course utilizing that right might result in the defeat of the proponent's project.

However, what many developers fail to realize is that input from the public can actually improve projects, and even save money. For example, the Samanalawewa hydropower project proceeded before there were EIA regulations in Sri Lanka. Had the public been given the opportunity to comment, it might have informed the CEB, again the project proponent, that there was an underground tunnel from ancient limestone quarry in the vicinity of the planned reservoir. Instead, the CEB built the reservoir in ignorance of this fact, and consequently suffered substantial expense when the reservoir leaked into the tunnel. In contrast, when the public was offered the opportunity to comment on a later project, the massive Colombo-Katunayake Expressway project, the public offered some very good, low cost alternatives to the original design.

Other factors that affect public participation are the cost of the EIA reports and how they are written. In the first respect, these reports are generally expensive to obtain relative to the income levels of the local people affected. Copies of the reports should be made available for the cost of copying only and nothing more.

In the second respect, EIA reports must be made more understandable to the local people. Incredibly, the EFL has had to sue the government to force it to make EIA reports available in Sinhala, the dominant language of Sri Lanka, rather than in English, the common language of consultants. While the requirement that the EIA report be in a language that people can understand is obvious, it is surprising how often that this is a problem in developing countries. Moreover, care must be taken to insure that the translations are correct and complete. Since the requirement for Sinhala translations took effect in Sri Lanka, there have been instances where the translations were incorrect and important data was omitted. This problem could be ameliorated by allowing interested parties to extend or reopen the public comment period where omissions or inaccuracies are uncovered.

Once the obvious problem of translation is overcome, there is the more difficult issue of the reports' technical language (touched on above). The EIA report should be made clear to lay readers, rather than understandable by specialists only. Indeed, the need for this requirement has been recognized by the European Union, which mandates that all EIA reports in EC countries contain a non-technical summary of required information.[58] If this need is acknowledged for industrialized countries where literacy and technical training are high, it is all the more important in developing countries, where the mass of people lack technical training.

Another way in which public participation can be fostered is to invite all interested parties to scoping sessions which prepare the IEE/EIA terms of reference. Though the law in Sri Lanka is relatively advanced in *allowing* the public, and particularly NGOs, to attend scoping sessions, public involvement is still not welcome by most project approving agencies. If the public can participate before the terms of reference are prepared, then projects can be improved from the start, and possible opposition neutralized.

Additionally, improvements are needed to legal rights and remedies. A glaring inequity in the current Sri Lankan process is that project proponents can appeal after disapproval by either the PAA or the CEA, but project opponents do not have that reciprocal right. This inequity should be repaired.

Moreover, there is little provision currently in Sri Lankan law for monitoring approved projects for compliance with conditions of approval set by the PAA. At present, only the CEA can take legal action against a developer who is violating such conditions. That should be changed to allow legal action by the PAA, as well as by members of the public. Also, a system of self-monitoring by developers could be instituted (with periodic reporting), as well as the establishment of community monitoring committees. Such procedures by their very existence would improve compliance with legal requirements, and would relieve government of some of the burden of monitoring compliance.

Finally, the EIA process in Sri Lanka, like similar laws throughout the world, are unnecessarily limited to individual projects. The EIA process should also be applied strategically to industrial sectors and geographical regions of the country. A powerful argument in support of this approach is the environmental damage of the Mahaweli regional development project, of which the UKHP was but a small part. As mentioned above, the massive Mahaweli project has had devastating effects on the environment of southeast Sri Lanka, with few of the anticipated rewards. It was launched by Sri Lanka and the World Bank without enough strategic thought of the environmental consequences. Though the World Bank now required EIAs on all newly-funded projects, it still does not require its projects to be subject to strategic or regional EIAs.

2. Government Attitude in the Implementation of the EIA Process

As is demonstrated on a daily basis throughout the developing world, good laws accomplish nothing because they are not properly implemented. A common cause of failure is the lack of institutional commitment on the part of some government officials. One symptom of this problem is an arrogance towards the public and NGOs. While the arrogance of bureaucrats is an inherent consequence of power, it undermines a process whose very purpose is to foster public participation and power sharing. In Sri Lanka, this attitude by some officials can be manifested by small deceits, such as the practice in some rural offices of hiding EIA reports from the public. Or, the attitude can take the form of simply failing to inform the public on how it can comment on a project or failing to invite the public to a scoping session. No matter what form it takes, the lack of commitment on the part of government officials enervates the process in Sri Lanka, a problem which is undoubtedly present in other developing countries.

A related problem is bias in favour of projects on the part of government officials, and particularly officials within the PAAs. While Sri Lanka's EIA regulations specify that the project proponent cannot also be the PAA, the PAA is generally the government agency most concerned with the project. Though actual bias on the part of the concerned agency is difficult to prove in most instances, such bias was only too obvious in the Ministry of Power and Energy's decision to approve the UKHP over the recommendations of its TEC and in its urging the CEA to approve the project on technical and economic grounds alone.[59] More problematic is the inherent conflict of interest of project approving agencies where they have authority to approve projects in which they have a policy interest.

One suggestion for reducing bias is to have one, central authority approve all projects pursuant to the EIA process. The decisions of this office should still be confirmed by another office such as the CEA in order to maintain the safeguard of a concurring agency. No doubt this approach can be criticized on the grounds that a single agency would lack the expertise that the concerned agency brings to the evaluation of all projects within its jurisdiction. However, educating decision-makers in a central authority is already done for officials of the CEA, so one more set of officials would be only marginally more work. The real concern in making this change is the difficulty of assembling the necessary political power to deprive the PAA from jurisdiction over approving new power projects. Alternatively, one could increase the education of government participants in the EIA process. Such education would include communication that describes and promotes the EIA process generally. In this way, public officials could gain greater respect for the process and greater sensitivity to all the competing concerns.

3. Educating the Public

However information and training to operate the EIA process is needed by other participants in the EIA system. This need has been recognized in Sri Lanka and is being partially met by a joint effort by the University of Peradeniya and the Natural Resources and Environmental Policy Project (a long-term environmental assistance project undertaken by the Sri Lankan government and USAID). These groups sponsor a training course for consultants, government officials, industrialists and some academics. However, the course is held periodically in expensive hotels and costs approximately US $40,000 per course.

A more effective approach would be to save the money on the fancy hotels and provide grass-roots education in more humble environs for a greater number of people. Surely, representatives of government and industry can learn just as well in simpler surroundings. More importantly, there is wide-spread ignorance of the EIA process by the public generally. Since the public at large has a role to play in the process, they should receive education along with the other participants. Therefore such training courses should at least be open to the public.

A legitimate concern toward opening such sessions up to the public is that since most members of the public lack technical training they might not understand the presentations of experts at training sessions for government and industry. This may well be so for the majority of people but this should not foreclose the option for other members of the public.

For the rest of society, some rather simple measures can be taken. First, public service announcements on radio are a familiar means of educating the public on other issues in many developing countries. They could just as easily be used for informing people of the existence of the right to comment on development projects. Another means of background education should include teaching the fundamentals of the process to older children in the schools. Not only would this educate large numbers of future citizens, but the information would filter on to parents and relatives. Furthermore most importantly since the mass of people are seldom concerned with their rights until something happens to make those rights relevant, there should be public education in association with prescribed projects. For example, project proponents should be required to advertise the publication of their EIA reports in advance of making those reports available, so as to give people time to prepare themselves to comment. This could be done by a program roughly similar to the one employed by the EFL and other NGOs during the UKHP campaign, that is through leaflets and posters. As those NGOs have shown, such publicity need not be expensive. Additionally, a minimum of one and perhaps two training sessions on how to comment should be held in the affected area, and borne at the expense of the project proponent. There is evidence that in the case of the UKHP, representatives of the CEB and its consultants spent considerable time in the Talawakelle area talking to local villagers during preparation of the EIA without actually informing them fully about the upcoming UKHP. Surely, if project proponents have entered areas to gather information on the environmental and social impacts of projects, it is no great burden to require them to explain to local people what they plan to do and of the people's rights to comment.

Without doubt, the proposals for public education suggested here would be met with considerable resistance by government and industry. Though these measures would not add measurably to the cost of large projects such as the UKHP, they add inconvenience and uncertainty. The last thing that a project promoter wants to do is to delay the project as it reaches the final approval stage, or to empower forces that might defeat the project's approval. Nevertheless, the EIA process is not simply about approving or disapproving projects. The process is equally about rigorously examining alternatives so that the government is satisfied that the project has been designed to balance technical, financial, social and environmental factors in the best conceivable way. Inevitably, any project proponent has considered such factors and struck a balance to maximise its interests. These decisions, often involving important tradeoffs, should be critically examined by government decision-makers to see that the balance is fairly struck for all concerned. The result of that examination need not be the disapproval of the project if the project proponent has struck the balance too heavily in its favour, but rather an adjustment of the balance. Indeed, most elements in developing countries eagerly support development, and so are happy to see large projects proceed. Therefore, educating the public on their right to comment on projects should not be a hindrance at all.

Conclusion

The principles that government should act to minimize the environmental impacts of development and that the public should have a direct role in that decision-making process are two of the greatest contributions of American environmental law. These are worthy principles that have been embraced almost universally in recent years among countries throughout the world. However, adaptation of the legal procedures implementing these principles poses special difficulties in developing countries. The reasons are manifold. Fundamental imbalances of power tilt in favour of developers and against the EIA process functioning as designed. Ignorance, bias, and even corruption frequently possess government decision-makers. And fundamentally, people in developing countries, especially rural people, lack the traditions of western democracies where the EIA process was forged. Considering all these necessities, it sometimes seems that only through the confluence of fortuitous circumstances that the EIA process works at all.

Be that as it may, these problems are not insurmountable if the circumstances in the country are benevolent. First and foremost, there must be a free press and a political situation that allows public protest. Second, the EIA process must be transparent and participatory, with responsible public officials at some point in the process to check that the EIA law is being implemented as intended. Third, there must exist competent NGOs who are free to lead opposition to such projects.

Once these preconditions are met, opposition to the project must go forward on dual tracks. First, compelling technical arguments must be presented in written form which show that the project has unacceptable or unnecessary environmental impacts. Further, public pressure on the government must be generated through carefully organized campaigns in the media and at the grass-roots level. Of crucial importance in this latter task is effective leadership which discovers and investigates new development projects, informs local people of the existence and impact of such projects, and teaches them about their rights and how to exercise them. This public aspect of the EIA process is so important because it is a fact of life that the forces mentioned above (e.g., imbalances of power) are constantly at play to bend government decision-making in their favour. However, people with opposing views can force a balanced review of the issues in a development project if they create the situation where the decision will be made under public scrutiny. The latter can be achieved by informing people of the issues and encouraging them to speak out. For ultimately, even in socially stratified countries, power rests with the people and if the people demand justice, justice will be done.

Notes

1. The Economist Intelligence Unit, Sri Lanka Country Forecast, August 7, 1995.

2. Demand for Electricity in Sri Lanka is Increasing at a Rate of About 10 Per Cent a Year, Lloyds List at p.8 (March 28, 1984). In 1995, the Independent Power Report found taht the demand grew at a rate of 7.2% over the previous 20 years. Sri Lanka Seeks Private Sector Help for 1,840 MW; SOme Sceptical, Independent Power Report at p.14 (September 8, 1995).

3. Sri Lanka Seeks Private Sector Help for 1,840 MW; Some Sceptical, Independent Power Report at p. 14 (September 8, 1995).

4. According to Deputy Conservator of Forests, K.P. Ariyadasa. "50 Percent of Forest Cover Lost in Sri Lanka" Xinhua General Overseas News Service, March 28, 1992.

5. Thosapala Hewage, Sri Lanka's Director of Forestry Planning. "Sri Lanka-Environment: Missing the Woods for the Trees", by Rita Sebastian. Inter Press Service, February 2, 1995. This view was shared by K.P. Ariyadasa, Deputy Conservator of Forests, who attributes the loss to "large-scale agricultural expansion and irrigation schemes." "50 Percent of Forest Cover Lost in Sri Lanka" Xinhua General Overseas News Service, March 28, 1992.

6. Thosapala Hewage, Sri Lanka's Director of Forestry Planning. "Sri Lanka-Environment: Missing the Woods for the Trees", by Rita Sebastian. Inter Press Service, February 2, 1995.

7. Mahaweli River Development Project, "Yesterday, Today and Tomorrow" (June 1992).

8. "Environmental aspects were neglected. Economic returns were lower than expected, farmers remain dependent on the government, and maintenance has been inadequately managed and funded," say the authors of the performance audit report on the Bank's funding of the Mahaweli project. Pratap Chatterjee, ENVIRONMENT: U.N. HELPING TO DESTROY WORLD'S RIVERS, SAY CRITICS, Inter Press Service (June 21, 1995).

9. Hemantha Withanage, "Environmental Impact Assessment Process - A White Elephant?", The Island (September 13, 1995).

10. Though Victoria Falls were rather modest in height, only 11 metres high, Lakshapana Falls were 126 metres high and connected to one of Sri Lanka's religious legends. The waters from the Laksapana Falls rise from a point called Indikatupana (indikatu means needles and pana means lamp). An old story tells that Lord Buddha

once sat on a rock at the Indikatupana to repair his clothes. Pilgrims still stop there on the way to Sri Lanka's highest point (Adams Peak) to sew material with a needle and thread.

11. Sri Lankan Ambassador to the United Nations, Stanley Kalpage. Quoted in Sri Lanka: "Shoot on Sight" Order for Felling Trees., by Thalif Deen Inter Press Service, April 2, 1992.

12. Sri Lanka: "Shoot on Sight" Order for Felling Trees, by Thalif Deen, Inter Press Service, April 2, 1992.

13. The EIA provision in the Coastal Conservation Act authorized an EIA process for coastal development only.

14. William A. Tilleman, "Public Participation in the Environmental Impact Assessment Process: A Comparative Study of Impact Assessment in Canada, the United States and the European Community", 33 Colum. J. Transnat'l L. 337 (1995).

15. "Sri Lanka-Environment: Missing the Woods for the Trees", by Rita Sebastian. Inter Press Service, February 2, 1995.

16. *Ibid.*

17. Forestry Minister D.M. Jayaratne. "Sri Lanka-Environment: Missing the Woods for the Trees", by Rita Sebastian. Inter Press Service, February 2, 1995.

18. Act 56 of 1988 added Part IV C pertaining to Approval of Projects to the National Environmental Act of 1980.

19. Final Decision of Secretary Cecil Amerasinghe, Ministry of Transport, Environment and Women's Affairs, August 3, 1995, in regard to the Appeal of the Ceylon Electricity Board against the refusal to approve the Upper Kotmale Hydropower Project, at page 11 (hereinafter "Appeal Decision").

Indeed, in resolving the appeal of the CEB of the rejection of the Upper Kotmale Hydro Project, Secretary Amerasinghe of the Ministry of Transport, Environment and Women's Affairs cited exclusively to United States cases and other American legal authorities in interpreting Sri Lankan law.

20. Id at 12. It has also been emphasized by Sri Lanka's environment ministers that early consideration of alternatives and public participation are at the heart of the EIA process: "The usefulness of an EIA increases if the process is integrated from an early stage into the planning and design of a project . The earlier the process is integrated the greater the chance that the project siting and design would be the best alternative ..." Id at 11 (emphasis in the original).

21. Regulations of the Minister of Environment and Parliamentary Affairs under Section 23CC of the NEA, No. 47 of 1980. Gazette Extraordinary of the Democratic Socialist Republic of Sri Lanka - June 24, 1993. (Hereinafter "EIA Regulations") (See Appendix B).

22. The EIA Regulations do set a minimum threshold for Prescribed Projects, though those minimums are quite small. For example, any conversion of forest to non-forest use of over 1 hectare is covered. EIA Regulations, June 24, 1993.

23. Smith and van der Wansem, "Strengthening EIA Capacity in Asia: Environmental Impact Assessment in the Philippines, Indonesia, and Sri Lanka", at p. 51; World Resources Institute (June 1995) (hereinafter "Smith and van der Wansem"). The failure by Sri Lanka to used the EIA process for strategic planning is a common criticism of the EIA process in Asia. Id. at p. 19.

24. Compare, for example, the breadth of prescribed projects under Sri Lanka's EIA regulations with the current EIA Directive of the European Community, EEC 85/337. The EC's EIA Directive requires that only major listed projects and projects having "significant" impacts are subject to EIAs. Member States of the EC have

wide discretion to determine whether a project's impacts are "significant." So, for example, a housing development in the United Kingdom involving 3,700 new homes on 250 hectares was determined by the British government not to be "significant." See, Wm. R. Sheate, Making an Impact: A Guide to EIA Law & Policy, at 31 (Cameron May). In contrast, a project of only 1,000 units or which involves clearing only 50 hectares is covered by the EIA Regulations in Sri Lanka. EIA Regulations, Part I(5) and (10).

25. The work of the CEA and PAAs is further facilitated (and to some extent complicated) by a number of other committees. There is the EIA Inter-Agency Committee which reviews the EIA process, further advises the PAAs, and is supposed to integrate EIAs into national policy. There is also an EIA Oversight Committee within each PAA which has ultimate approval authority over each project. Additionally, each PAA also has an "EIA Cell" which is responsible for administering the EIA process within that agency. And finally, PAAs typically appoint a temporary Technical Evaluation Committee to advise it on the technical aspects of each project requiring approval. CEA Guidance for IEE/EIA Process (1993).

26. Terms of Reference is the common term for a detailed description of the impacts to be studied in the IEE or EIA reports.

27. While public comment on a project prior to the approval/disapproval decision is common to EIA procedures throughout the world, participation at the scoping stage is not. For example, while it is acknowledged by scholars that the public should be given an opportunity to have input into the scoping process, it is seldom done. Wm. R. Sheate, "Amending the EC Directive (85/337/EEC) on Environmental Impact Assessment", at p. 77, European Environmental Law Review (March 1995) (hereinafter "Sheate, European Environmental Law Review"). Currently, this right is not a feature of the EIA process in the United States, Canada or the United Kingdom, and it is not a requirement of Member States of the European Community. Wm. R. Sheate, Making an Impact: A Guide to EIA Law & Policy, (Cameron May). For example, the EC's EIA Directive does not provide for public participation in scoping, but requires only that the public be "informed" of the environmental impacts of a project before the project is "initiated." This feature of Sri Lankan law is rather progressive by comparison.

It should be noted, however, that the EC Commission has proposed amendments to 85/337/EEC that would provide for public participation in scoping. However, as of the date of publication, the EC's Member States have yet to adopt this revision, and even if the amendment is adopted, the Single European Act provides that Member States have three years in which to implement this change.

28. Section 33, NEA (1988).

29. Government notices are published in all three languages used in Sri Lanka - Sinhala, Tamil and English.

30. The Guidance states that a request for a public hearing is one factor for the PAA to consider in setting a hearing. Guidance for IEE/EIA Process, Central Environmental Authority. Colombo, Sri Lanka, 1993. Other factors mentioned in the guidance are whether the project is controversial, whether the project impacts important environmental areas, or whether it has unusual national or regional impacts. Nevertheless, a practice has developed that a simple written request by a recognized group, such as an NGO, is sufficient ground for the PAA to set a hearing.

31. In a recent case, a project proponent used this law to restrict entry to the public hearing. This is a legal issue currently being contested by the Environment Foundation, Ltd., the leading environmental NGO in the campaign against the UKHP.

32. Section 23DD(1), NEA (1988).

33. Appeal Decision at page 5.

34. Appeal Decision at p. 6.

35. A run of river project involves a series of small dams.

36. The Devon Oya, Pundal Oya, Puna Oya, Ramboda Oya, and Andrew Oya. Oya is the Singalese term for a small tributary of a river.

37. The UKHP was the second dam project on the Kotmale River. Previously, in 1986, the CEB constructed the Lower Kotmale dam (134 MW), about 15 kilometers down river of the proposed Talawakelle site. The dam was constructed in an earthslide area where soil erosion is very high. There was no assessment of the environmental impacts of the project, and no serious opposition to its construction.

38. "CNEC" stands for a consortium of four organizations: the Chuo Kaihatsu Corporation, Nippon Koei Co., Ltd, EPDC International Ltd. (all of Tokyo, Japan), and the Central Engineering Consultancy Bureau (Sri Lanka).

39. This was decided by the PAA for the project, the Ministry of Power and Energy.

40. River flows would be stopped to the three major falls, Devon Falls (97 meters), St. Claire major (80 m) and St. Claire minor (50 m) falls, during all but selected periods. The smaller waterfalls of the Ramboda, Pundal, St. Andrews, Holyrood and Puna oyas would also be substantially modified in their appearance and flow.

41. About 15 earth vibrations were recorded in this area after the construction of other Mahaweli reservoirs.

42. An earth slop occurs when soil on a steep slope cracks in the dry season and later slips during the rainy season. At present, a large piece of land, about 50 hectares, is sliding toward the Lower Kotmale reservoir.

43. 1992 World Bank study on the environmental impacts of the Mahaweli project.

44. "Assuming erosion at 333 m3/km2, the sediment load flowing into the Talawakelli reservoir will be about 100,000 m3/year, representing about 15% of the reservoir volume." UKHP Conceptual Design Report, Volume II, Supporting A Preliminary Environmental Impact Assessment Report, Section 6, p. 12 (March 1994).

45. Malaria increased downstream of reservoirs in the massive Mahaweli River irrigation project in southwest Sri Lanka.

46. Appeal Decision at p. 7.

47. Appeal Decision at p. 9.

48. Appeal Decision at p. 10.

49. The EFL dates from 1981.

50. The EFL has also taken a leading role in filling lawsuits to require the government to follow the EIA regulations.

   It should also be mentioned at the outset that the EFL's opposition to the UKHP, like these other projects, was not the result of an ideological opposition to development, but from its concern over bad development. Thus, when the EFL began its campaign against the UKHP, its goal was not necessarily to scuttle the UKHP altogether, but to defeat the unsound development alternative at Talawakelle.

51. The EFL worked with two other national NGOs, the Sri Lanka Environmental Journalist Forum and the Organization to Safeguard Life and Environment (OLSEN), and one local grass roots NGO, the Sinhala Tamil Rural Womens Organization.

52. In conjunction with its written comments, the EFL requested and obtained a public hearing at Nuwara Elyia, the regional centre of the Talawakelle area.

53. Appeal Decision at p. 9.

54. The Oversight Committee of the PAA was chaired by the Secretary to the Ministry of Power and Energy. It also included a representative from the Overseas Economic Co-operation Fund (OECF), which was to be a funder of the project. Having such a representative on the decision committee was a clear conflict of interest.

55. Appeal Decison at p. 15.

56. Appeal Decision at p. 16.

57. Appeal Decision at p. 17.

58. EC Directive No. 85/337/EEC.

59. An even clearer example of bias occurred during the EIA process surrounding the Colombo-Katunayake Expressway project. The PAA in that case, the Ministry of Transport and Highways, published advertisements actually *promoting* the project! When confronted with its obvious bias the ministry refused to relinquish its approval authority. The EFL eventually filed a lawsuit to have it removed as the PAA.

Part II - Introduction

Financial and Managerial Education

Deborah A Blackman
Principal Lecturer in Human Resources, Southampton Business School

Gin Chong
Research Leader, Southampton Business School, Southampton Institute

The importance of environmental issues on the political agenda has grown rapidly within the UK over the last ten years. As a result the issues are firmly within the business and economic agenda and are referred to throughout all walks of life. Awareness is being raised from an early age via television programmes such as Blue Peter and Newsround which are targeted at the under 15 age group. They stress the need to care for the environment in which we live and to protect it for the future. The slogan of 'act local and think global' has now gradually been instilled into the minds of the general public.

The debate as to whether business should mirror education or vice-versa is on-going but there is no doubt that the subject is now to be found on curricula in primary and secondary schools, further and higher education institutions and within professional and organisational education programmes. This section of the book examines what should be taught, how and why at different levels of accounting, managerial and organisational education.

As pertains to accounting syllabi, environmental accounting and auditing have been included in all major accounting bodies in the UK. Universities and other teaching institutions have also incorporated such issues into their accounting and financial courses, whether delivered to accountants or other disciplines who need to have a financial awareness. However, there is still a lack of a proper guideline on how these environmental and ethical issues should be reported in the financial statements. Accountants are aware of these needs, but they are still in the midst of striving for the best methods of both addressing and presenting them.

The problem with management education is similar regarding the need to find a way to build environmental issues into the core decision-making framework of the potential manager. Whilst such issues are viewed almost as an 'optional extra' when learning is taking place the managerial instinct will not include them in the strategy setting framework. Ways of addressing this are outlined in the following chapters highlighting ways to integrate environmental teaching into the core syllabi and of enabling awareness to be part of the individual's core value set via deep cognitive understanding.

In chapter five Dr. Zhu defines the importance of educating about the environment per se. He identifies that part of the problem is that people are not taking the issue seriously enough and identifies some possible outcomes unless this ceases to be so. The need to educate at all levels to ensure that in future the environment is seen as key to our future is a recurring theme throughout the section and is underpinned by the model and examples introduced by Zhu. Paul Jarvis is looking specifically at the need for proper guidelines on environmental accounting and reporting. Without these education is inevitably going to be piecemeal as each lecturer will address the topic in a different and possibly contradictory manner.

Blackman & Fleming in chapter seven are stressing the need for management education to integrate environmental issues into mainstream management subjects if it is to be assumed into students' core knowledge which is used for decision-making. The growth in importance of managerial understanding outlined by Zhu is developed and ways forward identified for higher education.

The issue of integrating environmental education into the syllabi of accounting professionals is addressed by Helps in chapter eight. The importance of such issues to professionals is explored and their fundamental nature concluded in a recommendation that both environmental and ethical issues could be examined.

Chapter nine examines what organisations should be doing internally whilst they are awaiting the influx of educational awareness from future employees. The reality is that if organisations are to be able to act in an environmentally aware manner all employees must be committed to implementing the necessary strategy that enables this to happen. This will only happen if they understand not only the reasoning behind such strategies but also the best way to achieve such strategies.

A more specific micro view is taken by Jason Palmer and Rita Van Der Hurst in chapter ten where they are applying some of the ideas outlined earlier to the specific case of Small and Medium Sized Enterprises who have limited time and resources to spare. They would often argue that whilst it is all right for the large organisations to have costly staff development plans they can not realistically have such luxuries. The need to raise awareness is stressed once more as a learning strategy with the proviso that it must be linked to business activities to give it a feeling of importance.

The section overall highlights how the future of organisations (and our civilisation) necessitates new approaches to spreading knowledge and learning throughout the framework that designs, manages and audits our business world. That everyone must take responsibility at all levels is highlighted clearly and the implications of this for both management and employee development are shown to be very far reaching. Schools have taken the issue on board but in some cases this is the last time formal input takes place as people specialise within their jobs and spheres of influence. The importance of educating everyone involved within our organisations is made clear and a start is made on finding a way forward.

5 What Should We Bring Into Environmental Education?

Zhichang Zhu
Centre for Systems Studies, University of Hull

Introduction

The 1972 United Nations' Human Environment Conference in Stockholm highlighted a turning point in the environmental movement world-wide. Since then, the issue of environmental protection and sustainable development has become a central focus in public debates, in government policy/decision making, and in the conducting of organisational and individual behaviour, all over the world. Accordingly, environmental education and training has made remarkable progress, in the sense that it has increased public awareness and concern of environmental issues, translated such awareness and concern into conscious action, and made environmental protection an important criterion in decision making.

Environmental education remains, however, unsatisfactory since so far it mainly focuses on, and stops at, convincing people of the vitainess of environmental issues for everyone and for later generations, the importance of innovational technology strategies and programmes, and the necessity of environmental criteria in individual day-to-day behaviour, etc. While education as such has some significance, it nevertheless fails to stimulate and assist people to address the complexity involved in environmental decisions and actions. We know, through environmental education, that environment protection and innovational technology are vital for sustainable development and even for human survival. Even so, controversial projects still go ahead in spite of public protest, for example the recent Chinese Three Gorges Project in China and the French nuclear testing in the South Pacific. Are these projects necessary, inevitable, and urgent in terms of the enhancement of the human situation, compared with other needs such as reducing poverty and hardship which we can find everywhere world-wide? To answer these questions, what is lacking in our 'paradigm' of thinking and acting? In other words, what should we bring into our environmental education and training?

This paper suggests that our problem and incompetence may stem from reductionism in our current environmental thinking and education. That is, our environmental thinking and education have been exclusively constrained within the technical sphere only. While the technical consideration is an indispensable and important one, it is by no means a sufficient description of the whole issue. From a holistic point of view, the environmental issue has wid¯reaching impacts on all objective, subjective, and intersubjective aspects of human life on the one hand, and is conditioned by all those aspects on the other. We cannot therefore isolate the environmental issue from those aspects, but should sweep those aspects into our environmental thinking, decisions, actions and education.

To this end, this paper, drawing upon Habermas's communication thesis, constructs a conceptual model which tries to bring dimensions of technical improvement, mutual understanding, and human relations into environmental education. The model contends that as humans we live within a complex reality which is constituted by an objective natural world, a subjective internal world, and an intersubjective social world Therefore we have cognitive and action interests in objective truth, in mutual understanding, and in intersubjective social norms. To make rational and responsible environmental decisions, especially those in government policies, we have no other option but to bring those interests systemically into our thinking and procedure. Accordingly, environmental education and training should educate government officials, technical experts, business executives, and general citizens to think and act on all these aspects and the interdependency among them.

This paper is divided into two sections. The first section begins with a case study of the Three Gorges Project, analysing what was involved and what was missing in the debates and decisions on it. The second section introduces a model of a three-world complexity and a distinction between two types of rationality, which are to be incorporated into environmental thinking and education.

Case Study: The Three Gorges Project

To dam the Three Gorges has been a long-term ideal of the Chinese since the beginning of this century. Sun Yat-sen, the founder of modern China, first proposed the project in the 1920s. That was a time when the environment had not yet become a concern for society and a time when an undeveloped China began to recognise the power of science and technology. Without experience of, or knowing about, the negative impacts of big dams, it was believed that modern hydraulic engineering, particularly large-scale multi-purpose dams, would control flooding, generate hydroelectricity, and improve navigation. It was also a time when the Chinese had just released themselves from the millennia-long rule of their 'Gods on the earth', the emperors; therefore, few of them expected that authorities or government would listen to them.

Since then, throughout the modern history of China, in spite of numerous interruptions by war, economic troubles and ideological struggles, continuous effort has been put into the Three Gorges Project by the central Government (both the Kuo-Ming-Dang and the communists), with the involvement and assistance, first of American dam-building agencies and then of Russian experts. Although exclusively focusing on technical considerations, and although most were in favour of the project, leaders of modern China, until recently, generally held that the Three Gorges Dam would be built, but not immediately; and that the project needed more careful and detailed studies and should be determined by scientific and democratic decision-making procedures.

The latest wave of efforts pushing the project ahead began in the late 1970s, not long after the 1972 United Nations Stockholm Conference. The two-decade-long study and debate has involved national and international participants: governments (the Chinese, the American, the Canadian, etc.), financial agencies (the World Bank, the Asian Development Bank, etc.), dam-building utilities and corporations (the U.S. Bureau of Reclamation, the U.S. Army Corps of Engineers, the American Consulting Engineers Council, the Canadian International

Development Agency, Acres International, Lavalin International, Hugro-Quebec International, the British Columbia Hydro International, etc.), dam-building equipment suppliers (the Danes, the Germans, the Americans, etc.), scientists, academics, environmental protection organisations, and so on.

Advocates of the big dam assert that the project is safe, environment enhancing, and beneficial in terms of the net profit calculated from power generating, navigation improvement, resettlement, and investment. Opponents argue that the plan for resettlement is unrealistic; that the project will produce negative impacts to the environment, for example generating earthquakes and landslides, thus being environmentally degrading; that the dam is not safe, is not satisfactory, in terms of flood control, sedimentation and navigation; that it is not beneficial for investment given the record of delays in Chinese construction (for example the Gezhouba, another dam on the Yangtze of a small scale, was delayed six years and cost double the budget to be completed), etc.[1,2].

A point in the debate which is worth highlighting is whether there exist alternatives for the big dam. While the CYJV study asserts that 'The Three Gorges Project will be the only economical way significantly to increase flood protection in the middle reaches of the Yangtze' (1), information from other sources questions this exclusive rationale. A thorough reading of those materials suggests that alternatives might exist and have comparative advantages in terms of power generating, farmland submerging, resettlement, safety, technical and financial requirements, etc.[3].

Several events which occurred during the period of the debate have significance for our discussion in this paper:

•   In 1981, American specialists were invited to the Three Gorges site and the U.S. Government began to provide technical assistance to the project according to a Sino-American agreement;

•   In 1983, the Yangtze Valley Planning Office under the central Government completed a feasibility study, recommending that a 175-metre-high dam be built with construction beginning in 1986;

•   In 1984, the State Council approved the project 'in principle' and proposed adopting it into the Seventh Five-Year Plan (1986-1990);

•   In 1985, the U.S. Three Gorges Working Group submitted a proposal favouring the project to the Chinese Ministry of Water Resources and Electric Power;

•   In 1986, the Economic Construction Group of the Chinese People's Political Consultative Committee concluded, after a 38-day field investigation, that 'The Three Gorges Project should not go ahead in the short term';

- In 1987 and 1988, the Chinese Academy of Sciences published collected papers on their research, conducted by the State Science and Technology Commission from 1983 to 1986, expressing their questions and countermeasures;

- In 1989, a collection of interviews and essays critical of the project, *Changjiang Changjiang! (Yangtze Yangtze!)*, was published in China;

- In January 1989, the then Vice Premier Yao Yilin announced at the spring session of the National People's Congress that the project should be postponed and that 'people do not need to spend too much energy debating this issue for the time being';

- At the same time, the Chinese People's Political Consultative Committee criticised the Chinese feasibility study as not having been conducted in a scientific and democratic manner, calling for a completely new study of the project;

- In February 1989, the Canadian International Development Agency (CIDA) announced completion of *The Three Gorges Water Control Project Feasibility Study*, claiming that a 185-metre high dam is technically, environmentally, and economically feasible, recommending that the project should go ahead;

- On June 4, 1989, the Tiananmen Square event happened;

- In June 1990, Premier Li Peng called for a revived deliberation on the project;

- In February 1992, the International Water Tribunal in Amsterdam criticised the Canadian feasibility study and suggested that the project should be halted until 'the rights of the people of the Yangtze Valley are respected';

- In April 1992, the National People's Congress officially approved the project;

- In 14 December 1994, 'after 40 years feasibility study', Premier Li Peng officially 'kicked off' the construction of the world's biggest dam on the building site, with 'actual preparation work begun two years ago'.

Now the big dam is being constructed. Some believe and are happy to see that the megaproject is becoming 'irreversible', while others question the 'irreversibility' and continue their campaign to stop it. Due to the long construction period and the huge amount of investment required (an estimated 17 years and 95.4 billion *Yuan* at the 1993 price level, according to official figures)[4], and due to uncertainties in the on-going debate and in international relations, the fate of the big dam remains to be seen.

Whatever fate the big dam may have, to go ahead or to stop, to be completed or to be abandoned, critical and significant issues have nevertheless been raised from the debate, from which lessons can be drawn for further desirable, responsible and viable decisions on the project and beyond. To analyse what has been involved and what has been missing in the debate and decisions on the project, this paper suggests that we should give attention to the following issues.

First, all parties involved in the debate claim that they adopted rational criteria of environmental protection/enhancement and followed scientific procedures and standards, yet we see great varieties and conflicts in their calculations and conclusions. Even among the advocates of the project, their studies usually lead to different recommendations, leaving concerned people with huge question marks and anxiety. For example, should the dam be 150, 175, 180, or 200 metres-high as recommended by different studies? What criteria have been considered and in what order? Obviously, to answer these questions and make decisions which have wide reaching and 'irreversible' impacts, rigorous scientific knowledge and sophisticated skills are vital and indispensable. Thus we have cognitive and action interests in technical improvement and 'objective truth'.

Next, environmental and relevant issues such as development cannot speak for themselves. It is human beings that conceive and express situations and manipulate data for decision making. Even if all parties are faithful and serious in the regard of environment enhancement, sustainable development and democratic decision making, their definition and understanding of all these criteria or issues might vary greatly, due to cultural and ideological differences. While the International Water Tribunal in Amsterdam suggested that the Three Gorges Project should be halted until 'the rights of the people of the Yangtze Valley are respected'[1], an official of the Yangtze Valley Planning Office asserted that 'it's out of the question to ask people if they want to be moved or to consult with them'[5], which gives us a good example of differences in cultures, ideologies, and polities. More often than not, what seems sustainable or rational to some parties may not appear so to some others. Furthermore, under spoken declarations and assertions, there might lie some other unspoken but deep-seated beliefs and rationales, for example, a belief that building the world's biggest dam would increase the confidence and sense of pride of the nation, etc. We therefore have cognitive and action interests in improving mutual understanding, to understand different definitions of relevant concepts and criteria, and to understand different cultural and ideological forces that condition and influence environmental decisions.

Finally, desirable, responsible, and viable environmental decisions can only be possible through open debate within appropriate human relationships. People in China have immediate and sad experiences of 'efficient' political power and inappropriate human relations which conditioned and determined environmental and ecological decisions (recall, for example, the debate between Chairman Mao Tse-tong and Professor Ma Ren-chu on the population policy in China and its consequence: in the 1950s, when Professor Ma of the Beijing University, based on his population model, challenged Mao's then policy which aimed at increasing China's population at a large scale, Mao denounced Ma and his colleagues as right wing and anti-revolutionist, simply packed them off first into labour camps then into prison. During the subsequent silence, China's population tripled within 40 years. For an analysis of the debate, see for example the author's forthcoming paper: Learning from Man-made Disasters). These experiences, with their wide-reaching impacts, remind us that, confronted with decisions which have impacts on all citizens and later generations, no singular rationale, whether it comes from experts or authorities, can be complete or comprehensive. Every voice should be heard with equal attention and respect, and should be given equal consideration, which is the quintessence and precondition of science and democracy. Unlike the days of Sun Yat-sen, nowadays people want to express their concerns and want to be involved in decision making. They want a better decision-making environment and procedures, and they have rights to them. Thus, we have cognitive and action interests in improving intersubjective relations.

In summary, to make desirable, responsible, and viable environmental and ecological decisions, we human beings have accountability and interests in technical improvement, in mutual understanding, and in intersubjective relations. As a logical requirement, environmental education should bring all these aspects, not just technological issues, to the endeavour, so that government officials, technical experts, business executives, and ordinary citizens have appropriate training and necessary skills to participate, to discuss, and to make decisions, so as to protect and enhance the environment and ecology.

A Model of Reality and Rationality

In the last section it was suggested that in environmental thinking and action we humankind should have accountability in technical improvement, in mutual understanding, and in human relations for responsible decision making, and that therefore we should bring all these aspects into environmental education. This suggestion can be linked to, and supported by, a model of a three-world reality and a distinction between two types of rationality. This section will focus on introducing such a model, which is adopted from Habermas's communicative action theory[6,7].

According to Habermas, our reality can be conceived as being constituted of three interdependent worlds, and accordingly we should develop differentiated knowledge and methods to tackle issues arising in these three worlds. Firstly, we can have a natural world complexity, which consists of 'objective phenomena'. Dealing with such objective phenomena, e.g., investigating the natural conditions of the Three Gorges and relevant areas, studying feasibility and costs of resettlement, calculating power generating capacity, deciding how high the dam should be if it is to be built, comparing the Three Gorges proposal and other possible alternatives, etc., we must follow mechanisms of natural movements or law-like generations. Ignoring this objective world or downplaying those mechanisms would inevitably produce disasters, which has been proved by the negative impacts and unestimated limitations of previous projects such as the world's big dams.

Second, we can have an internal world complexity, with which we try to make sense of various validity claims in decisions or proposals through others' perspectives as well as our own. This complexity is indispensable since recognition of objective phenomena depends on the existence of multiple subjectivities. It is not surprising that at different stages of development, confronted with different situations, 'sustainable', 'rational', or 'appropriate' can have different meanings for different people. There can be no absolute standards or ready answers, as to what consideration dimensions and criteria should be brought into a project or granted priority. For those of us who are discussing environmental issues sitting in an air-conditioned room, there is no question that 'small is beautiful', that 'green should not be evaluated by price', etc., while for those who have nothing left in their kitchens for this evening, or those who have no kitchens at all, immediate survival may sound more urgent, desirable, and rational than long-term sustainability or development promises. No sustainability imposed from outside can be sustainable. We also have experiences in this regard from numerous aid projects in the third world. To encourage and assist mutual understanding, 'scientific technology' simply cannot help since human desires or feelings cannot be reduced to or manipulated as objective 'facts'. Accordingly, this complexity is better dealt with by interpretive-hermeneutic methods[8,9].

Finally, we can have a social world complexity, which defines and conditions our conduct in relationships of value judgements, and within which we have to decide how values and judgements can be normatively constructed and interact. Understanding and tackling this third complexity is vital if we desire to achieve a higher level of criticisable rational agreement on our varying or conflicting subjective cognition about the natural world and about appropriate actions to take. The natural world and the subjective world are so complex and dynamic that no singular rationale or position can provide a complete and comprehensive description of them. Only through collective complementation among varying rationalities can we hope to be able to obtain feasible and viable decisions. Dealing with the intersubjective world, 'scientific technology', however advanced or sophisticated, is not appropriate, nor can we appeal to power or ideology. What we need is free debate without compulsion within which each party, involved or affected, is willing and able, and has equal chances and resources, to participate.

It is these three facets and the interdependency among them that constitute our 'reality', which can be called ontological complexity. This complexity conditions our discussion and decisions on environment and ecology, especially those about big projects and/or those in government policies/decision making. To obtain possible agreements or desirable decisions, we have to come up with statements on all these three 'worlds': i.e., a statement of truth (about objective phenomena), a statement of rightness (about what should be normatively accepted), and a statement of subjective understanding (about the orientation of specific subjectivity).

To tackle adequately this three-world complexity, Habermas distinguishes two types of actions and rationalities: those oriented to 'success' - the efficient achievement of ends, and those oriented to mutual understanding about those ends through critical dialogue; i.e., instrumental rationality/actions and communicative rationality/actions. Thompson has expressed Habermas's notion of rationality thus:

> When we use the term 'rational', observes Habermas, we assume that there is a close connection between rationality and knowledge. We assume, it seems, that actions or symbolic expressions are 'rational' insofar as they are based on knowledge which can be criticised. In calling an action 'rational' we may presume that the actor knows, or has good reason to believe, that the means employed will lead to success; in calling an expression 'rational' we may presume that it bears some relation to the world and hence is open to objective - that is, inter-subjective - assessment. The former case, by linking the term 'rational' to the notion of action oriented to success, offers an intuitive basis for what Habermas calls 'cognitive-instrumental rationality'. The latter case links

the term 'rational' to the notion of inter-subjective assessment and thereby points towards a broader concept of communicative rationality in which various participants overcome their merely subjective views and, by virtue of the mutuality of rationally motivated conviction, assure themselves of both the unity of the objective world and the inter-subjectivity of their life relations[10] (p. 282).

Thus, according to Habermas, communicative action, and in our case decision making on environmental issues, can be viewed and claimed as rational only when our mutual understanding and agreement are formed through non-manipulative and non-coercive argumentation which is itself 'built into' our everyday pre-theoretical life:

> We use the term argumentation for that type of speech in which participants thematise contested validity claims and attempt to vindicate or criticise them through arguments. An argument contains reasons or grounds that are connected in a systematic way with the validity claim of problematic expression. The 'strength' of an argument is measured in a given context by the soundness of the reasons; that can be seen in, among other things, whether or not an argument is able to convince the participants in a discourse, that is, to motivate them to accept the validity claim in question[6] (p. 18).

It is important to point out that claiming that decision making is primarily communicative action does not deny or downplay technical or behavioural considerations. The 'truth' of Habermas's notion of communicative rationality and argumentation is to urge us to distinguish and then to ensure communicative rationality and instrumental rationality in social affairs and to rebuild proper relations between these two dimensions. Otherwise, as in the case of environmental decision making and education so far, communicative rationality is, more often than not, reduced to, and suppressed by, instrumental rationality.

The suggested model contends that in modern societies, decision making (on environmental issues or whatever) is not primarily 'goal-directed', nor is it 'efficiency'-oriented in priority. Rather, any validity claim brought into environmental thinking and actions is first and foremost ethical. On the one hand, the model emphasises the possibility that normative validity claims supposed by different accountabilities or parties should and can be open to empirical falsification and critical refutation, and can therefore be rationally defended and vindicated, as well as dialogically discussed and evaluated among participants. On the other hand, the model challenges governments, politicians and technical experts alike to create, maintain, and participate in public discourse. This demands that no one should be excluded, that all have rights to make claims and criticise others, and that the only norms valid are those regulating common interests.

Conclusion

Based on the model of a three-world complexity and two types of rationality, as well as based on experiences from debates and decisions of megaprojects such as the Three Gorges Dam, this paper suggests that environmental education should move beyond its current exclusive vision of the technological dimension towards a wider scope which covers all three aspects of our conceivable reality and ensures the two types of differentiable rationalities. According to this model, environment education should train people in all three categories of knowledge and skills: analytic-empirical sciences for predicting and control of objective complexity, interpretive-hermeneutic sciences for assisting mutual understanding, and critical sciences for creating better-ordered decision-making procedures and atmosphere.

The model suggested here does not claim to provide ready answers or guarantee desirable and viable decisions. Nevertheless, it tries to point out a direction for better environmental education and training through which humankind can increase its awareness and ability to question the partiality and selectivity which we bring into environmental decisions. This, therefore, preserves the hope of making our decisions more critical and rational.

Notes

(1) CIPM Yangtze Joint Venture (CYJV), *Three Gorges Water Control Project Feasibility Study*, 1989.

(2) Barber, M. and Ryder, G., (eds.), *Damming the Three Gorges: What Dam Builders Don't Want You to Know*, 2nd ed., Probe International, Earthscan Publications Limited, London and Toronto, 1993.

(3) *Xin Hua Wenzhai*, 3, 1983, p. 98, in Chinese.

(4) *Beijing Review*, 36 (46), 1994, p. 6.

(5) Crothall, G., "Peking to approve flooding of farms by hydroelectric project", *South China Morning Post*, 6 April 1991.

(6) Habermas, J., *The Theory of Communicative Action, vol. I: Reason and the Rationalisation of Society*, 1981a, translated by McCarthy, T., Beacon Press, Boston, 1984; London, Heinmann, 1984.

(7) Habermas, J., *The Theory of Communicative Action, vol. II: A Critique of Functionalist Reason*, 1981b, translated by McCarthy, T., Beacon Press, Boston, 1987.

(8) Gadamer, H., *Truth and Method*, 1960, translated and edited by Barden, G. and Cumming J., Seabury Press, New York, 1975.

(9) Bredo, E. and Feinberg, W., (eds.), *Knowledge and Values in Social and Educational Research*, Temple University Press, Philadelphia, 1982.

(10) Thompson, J. B., "Rationality and social rationalisation: An assessment of Habermas's theory of communicative action", *Sociology*, Vol. 17, 1983, pp. 278-95.

6 Environmental Education: Needs and Implications in Financial Training

Paul Jarvis
Senior Lecturer, Finance and Accountancy, Colchester Institute

Within the United Kingdom primary education has adopted study of the environment within the key stages, secondary education sector Environmental Education has been established as one of the National Curriculum's five cross curricular themes. Higher education, in the delivery of Degrees and Higher National Diplomas in Business Studies and Administration usually include the studies of business ethics and quality management although these are discrete studies, often with a managerial rather than a financial emphasis. Outside the education sector organisations are pursuing environmental reporting standards and the press and other media deliver the environmental message from a variety of perspectives. Young children through television programmes like Blue Peter and Newsround have been given a global awareness, a sense of environmental 'right and wrong', a perception of life, and corporate behaviour in particular, that was never apparent in earlier generations. It is hoped that these activities have raised the public awareness of the issues and debates that surround the topic and that over time a means to address the problems and opportunities presented will come forth. In the mean time the accounting profession is confronting a series of opportunities itself. The public are demanding more accountability and hard information on the impact of economies upon the environment and economists and accountants are pressed to find an acceptable currency or language in which to trade. The accounting profession is still endeavouring to recover its reputation from the fall in the late eighties and it is now having to provide solutions to three, and some might say intractable, areas of professional competence:

- Environmental Reporting, disclosure and compliance;
- Environmental Accounting, forecasting and costing;
- Environmental Auditing compliance and control.

The Corporate Report, 1975, outlined the responsibility of the reporting company to those parties interested in the financial accounts "to communicate economic measurements of and information about the resources and performance of the reporting entity useful to those having reasonable rights to such information".

Recently this relationship has been brought sharply into question by the activities of pressure groups and consumer groups alike. The Brent Spar crisis demanded a review of the notion of 'stakeholder' and their relationship with the reporting entity. Shell did not obtain sufficient support from the public for their claim that sinking the platform in the Atlantic was the scientifically satisfactory solution. The consumer took the ethical and environmental view that the dismantling onshore was more friendly to the environment. To achieve this end consumers across Europe were united in the boycott of Shell products. It is increasingly apparent from this event, and others like it, that success and profitability will gravitate towards those firms who best seem to balance the interests of all their current and future stakeholders. Many large corporations have developed the theme of the ethical consumer and see this as a way to enter, or gain advantage in, the market place. Treating environmental issues with due diligence will pay off.

The dominant green theme that pervades much of corporate reports owes much to this public display of worthiness. Token disclosure with a view to wooing the dissenter, as a tool for promoting and marketing an image, as a means of deflecting political pressure became prevalent in the first half of this decade.

> ...Pacific Gas and Electronic Company is a traditional gas and electric utility company. A major part of this company's output (17.7%) comes from nuclear plants....(PG&E) therefore, has a strong vested defensive interest in green reporting. An active and public display of its green credentials could be useful in deflecting anti-nuclear publicity......A special feature of the report, printed on recycled paper, is numerous photographs with a wildlife theme. In particular, the financial statements are bedecked with 27 small cameo sized photographs of endangered Californian species[1].

Regulation to protect the environment has increased in complexity and diversity in the decade and companies have had to come to terms with compliance. As well there has been a gradual acceptance that without the environmental controls there will not be a sustainable structure within which to operate. The common perception has been that environmental controls produce additional financial burdens on the company which will drive down profits, or erode the company's ability to compete in the market place.

More recently it has been recognised that there are different categories of costs associated with going green. Some measures do cost money and provide no return in the medium term. However these costs are often necessary to remain in business and are borne by all companies in an industry. These can often be passed on to the consumer.

Other costs can bring benefits either through the saving of energy or resources. Thirdly there are costs which can be seen as producing a competitive advantage in performance enhancement, in particular in the area of BS7750. This has become an important area for smaller and medium size companies as larger companies demand higher standards. B&Q have developed a very comprehensive environmental policy and action plan, which not only gives guidelines to suppliers, but support and a framework of operations both in the UK and abroad. For example they can save £400,000 by not putting cardboard packaging into general waste skips, and a further £400,000 by baling and selling it[2].

As a consequence of this changing perspective upon environmental costs in 1992 the Canadian Institute of Chartered Accountants published a report, Environmental Auditing and the Accounting Profession,[3] in which it was recognised that;

> The profession faces an unprecedented opportunity and challenge to respond to significant emerging needs and expectations arising from concerns to protect the environment for future generations. The profession has much to contribute in shaping

future mechanisms for environmental accountability - more than it sometimes realises, more than others may have previously realised.

As well as identifying the fact that going green can save money for the company the profession has realised that the duty of care to the reader of the financial accounts, and the true and fair view, demand that the problems of environmental liabilities be recognised and reported in the accounts. Given that 60% of shareholders are interested in the environmental policies and practices of the organisation they are investing in, two thirds of fund managers and financial journalists, and half of banking analysts, have a very specific concern in the nature of the investment's behaviour[4], a significant weight of consumers of financial and corporate information are demanding more output from the profession.

The United Kingdom Accounting Profession has recognised the importance of environmental liabilities and the Accounting Standards Board (ASB) has issued in January 1996 a discussion paper Statement of Provisions which, in a separate chapter, deals specifically with environmental issues. It is an area which has not been properly addressed and of all the areas of environmental reporting has had the least attention paid to it. The impact upon the reporting entity of undisclosed restitution work, of the costs of cleaning a tract of polluted land or water could be considerable. The length of time that the liability might sit in the balance sheet is also significant, and could span many generations. A further issue for debate is at what point should any liability for environmental repair be recognised. As soon as a project is started some commitment to repair and restitution must be made. At this point some liability should therefore be carried in the accounts of the organisation. Current policy is for this liability to accrue over the life of the operation. However the restitution costs for rectification of environmental damage could be fully due or fall liable the moment the operation starts. The Accounting Standards Board have published this discussion paper to apply the principles set out in Financial Reporting Statements 3, Reporting Financial Performance, and 7, Fair Values in Acquisition Accounting, to all other provisions, namely abandonment costs should be recognised in full at the outset, and should be capitalised as a cost and therefore charged to the Profit and Loss account over the useful life of the asset. One of the considerations or concerns in this practice is that by including an environmental liability in the accounts of the company it could be argued in a court of law that the company has accepted ownership of, or demonstrated proof that, they have a legal responsibility for an environmental liability, opening up litigation against the company. There is not only a problem regarding current environmental damage, but also the legacy of past actions or non-actions which have created contaminated sites. The UK Government moves towards the principle of "polluter pays" these may have more serious impacts upon company financial reporting in the future. Claims against corporate indemnity insurance policies will also increase and one suspects that the insurance industry is also concerned with 'gradual pollution' and are giving much credence and favour to the establishment of environmental controls and management systems within the client organisational structure.

In the fifth year's (1995) review of the Association of Chartered and Certified Accountants (ACCA) Promotion of Environmental Reporting annual competition it was observed that "the day of the green glossy is clearly over"[5]. This conclusion has been made based upon the "...serious, and praiseworthy, attempts to address the major environmental ramifications of corporate activity"[5]. Thorn EMI, who won the ACCA award for the second consecutive year, have taken care to define the user groups to whom the report is addressed. (See Thorn EMI 'Focus on the Environment 95')[6]. Whilst many of the targets and progress are measured in physical units there is considerable information on the costs and savings made to the Group by implementing environmental strategies.

Environmental Expenditure and Savings: £000s

	EMI	THORN	HMV	TRANSACTION	TOTAL
Capital Exp.	1,393.9	23.8	19.0	47.7	1484.4
Operating Costs	1,476.1	58.3	137.1	25.5	1697.0
Savings	275.2	346.5	19.0	4.4	645.1

Extracted from Thorn EMI 'Focus on the Environment 95'

It could be assumed that some of the savings made will be greater in the year of starting, some of the operating costs may diminish for the same reason, and the capital expenditure should have on going effects upon the Profit and Loss Account. However this is not necessarily the only view to take.

There are many benefits accruing to the environment from the activities of Thorn, and others that have been quantified in tons of emissions reduced; wastes recycled; solvents not consumed. These activities as reported do not enable comparison with other corporate activities of identifiable worth or value. How do we measure the impact on the environment of a reduction in solvents manufactured? The use of money as a measure or comparator creates a barrier in some debates. Some things are considered priceless and there is often a morality question about certain 'rights'. However some value does need to be attributed to events and actions to enable the relative merits of actions to be assessed. The situation is made worse by the abuse that corporations have made to Cost Benefit Analyses (CBA), by hiding behind the pretence or facade of CBA to give form and credibility to a contentious management decision. CBA endeavours to provide the methodology for making decisions about controversial issues that affect disparate social political or environmental groups associated with the planned activity.

However examples such as Ford's 1970's CBA model for the 'Pinto', "Fatalities associated with crash-induced fuel leakage and fires", with the cost valuation of a rubber grommet being compared with the outgoings caused by the immolation of customers, created a mistrust of the mechanism. This was exacerbated by the specific issue, the methodology of valuing the price of bereavement compared with a small charge to change a vehicle's manufacture. Ford had based the valuations on readily available actuarial data already used in the US law courts to determine damages in liability cases. The major issue is one of attributing value to that considered sacrosanct and inviolable. (Also some might say because Ford suppressed some of the information).

The difficulty arising from the translation of activities to an economic measure has been revisited by Environmental Impact Analysis. Winpenny[7] recognises that there are pros and cons in valuing the environment and environmental issues. In summary these are:

Supporting valuation:

> the environment is not free;
> the comparison of quantifiable and non-quantifiable focuses the debate;
> valuing items narrows the field for pure judgement;
> it gives a truer indication of economic performance;
> giving a more secure base for policies.

Opposed to valuation:

> valuing the non-quantifiable devalues the debate;
> CBA is cynically manipulated;
> valuation requires technical competence and data;
> different areas of business / countries have unique problems and the principles are not transferable.

Society, more particularly the pressure groups, have demanded however that consideration and value be given to the actions taken by industries and governments. Once accepting that value can be applied to all things their relative worth can be established. I do not wish to enter into the ethical debate about the value of intangibles, of morality and ethical perspective, the relative worth of life in one part of the world to another, BUT these are the issues that do need to be addressed and reconciled if we are to have credibility in the financial reporting of and decision making upon actions and activities that affect our environment. Many of the smokestack industries have given great consideration to accountability and transparency in environmental activities. Returning to the Brent Spar, Shell took the decision based upon scientific evidence that the safest route was to dump the Spar in deep sea. Greenpeace apparently made some errors and miscalculations in contesting this action and "..Shell believed the potential commercial damage from following the "scientific evidence" to dump at sea was far greater than the cost of reversing the decision"[8]. Dr Chris Fay, Chairman and Chief Executive, Shell U.K. Limited, talked of the complexities of the impact of people and human activity upon the environment in a short advertisement in the *Times Higher* of 31st May 1996, bannered "Not Black and White but shades of Green". The quote suggests that we have to decide how to prioritise, and to face the costs and consequences of our actions. Dr Fay further suggests that, although environmental science is complex and the construction of detailed risk evaluation is not easy the fact remains that we must work with the best decision making tools and education available to us.

The public perception of what is and what is not correct or desirable is notoriously fickle. The way that Greenpeace swayed public opinion against Shell is proof of that. Research reported in the *Times Higher* of 31st May[9] by J.D.Graham of the Harvard School of Public Health's Center for Risk Analysis has an interesting footnote. Surveying eight (possible) hazards and the public's response to them, identifies a striking correlation. The higher the confidence score of the potential hazard the more frequently it has been featured in the press over the last two years!

Story Count Compared to Public Perception of Hazard

Story count in

Press	4,867	4,246	2,541	1,986	1,134	897
Hazard risk	7.7	7.1	7.0	6.9	6.2	5.5

Confidence score

Graham, Harvard School of Public Health's Center for Risk Analysis

There is pressure on companies and on accountants to "go green". Some specialists argue that much of the evidence of the impact of particular events and problems is inconclusive, that much of the pressure comes from a public whipped up by a press in silly season. This reporting, or mis-reporting by the press causes additional problems in the construction of sensitive models to evaluate the impact of environmental projects.

> In many environmental impact assessment studies, more attention has been given to adverse impacts and their remedial measures rather than to a balanced analysis between adverse inputs and benefits. So much so that the neutral term 'impact' is now often used - and understood - as 'adverse' impact,...these are more conspicuous[10].

Changes in public perception will only come slowly. The changes mentioned in the National Curriculum will help but it is also the responsibility of the protagonists, and in this I include professional bodies, to raise the profile of the debate and to clarify the parameters and boundaries in which we operate. Many organisations will need to make changes to the management process, and a change to the mindset and to consider innovative change as opposed to change brought about by regulation. This is linked to issues of Total Quality Management (TQM) and other quality performance indicators, by the involvement of all staff in the operations of the organisation, Kaisen. The paper industry has been subject to strict regulation of chemical emission, such as sulphur dioxide and chlorine, and water pollution, as well as confined access to renewable raw materials. The American industries in general reacted to events, the Swedish have sought to create solutions, which has led to marketing of new environmentally friendly processes and products such as bleach free paper nappies.

Organisations, and professions within organisations, need to develop Environmental strategies that will enable the problems to be addressed. One of the fundamental problems emanates from this mind set that is adverse to change. Three stages of management can be identified; old management; reactive management and proactive management. The former has insufficient concern regarding environmental issues, the middle route is meeting compliance as and when required and the latter will challenge and push forward. Concomitant to this is the cost to the business.

Whilst it appears that the cost of doing nothing, the former route, is small there will eventually be a high charge, uncompetitiveness. As Thorn have shown developing an environmental strategy may be expensive in the outset but the benefits accruing will go on for a long time.

As means of ensuring the continuity of benefits from environmentally friendly activities the accountant can introduce to the business the environmental audit. This is a systematic and objective review of the impact of an entity upon the environment.

The purpose is to appraise the current practices the organisation is currently undertaking and to enhance the performance by introducing beneficial (cost effective) change. This can be by the elimination of waste or consumption of materials, changing or enhancing the processes to reduce usage or emissions, redesigning or refining the products and re-evaluating the environmental impact of the policies of the business. BS 7750 specifies the requirements for the development and maintenance of environmental standards, and has many areas in common with BS 5750. This quality standard had much of its roots in the information already held in the accounts department, and once again accountants with their knowledge of all areas of an organisation, and the control of its management information flows should be in a strong position to help in the implementation of the procedures.

As with BS 5750 there is likely to be a cascade effect from the large customer through to the smaller supplier. B&Q recognises that the improved environmental performance produces better quality products which will lead to greater customer satisfaction. Each supplier will be given a classification based upon quality and environmental criteria, ranging from 'exceptional' to 'problem supplier'. The latter will have no new products stocked until they have resolved the problem issues[2]. Here then the environmental audit is not being conducted in house but by an outside agency, and critically the future performance of the business depends on meeting the success criteria of the customer. A case of change and adapt to stay still, but those changes do bring other benefits.

From an accounting perspective the issues relating to the environment can be broken down into the three areas considered at the start of this paper: Environmental Reporting, Environmental Accounting and Environmental Auditing. Valuation of land and resources and the disclosure of this valuation, either as a long term asset or liability, the treatment of the business risks and the avoidance of penalties and fines from the non compliance with reporting and environmental requirements. Increasing public awareness will mean that developments in disclosure, in new concepts of valuation must take place, and be seen demonstrably to have taken place. Cost streamlining, product process enhancement and product quality will flow from the generation of sound environmental accounting procedures and this will lead to customer satisfaction and retention. With the accounting systems comes the development of better management information systems bringing to the attention of management pertinent information to integrate the environmental data into the daily operating decisions. This may sound an altruistic aim, but reconsider the Corporate Report and the definition of the user groups and it is increasingly apparent that the most successful and profitable firms will be those that can reconcile the disparate interests of the various stakeholders whilst preserving their identity and reputation as caring and green.

We, as members of the profession, providing information to management to formulate policy, enabling investment decisions to be made, disclosing the results of the actions and activities, should be considering more environmental training for both our technicians and professional members, or we are likely to find the market place has been moved, or taken, away from us by engineers and specialist environmental consultants. As professionals already trained in the area of financial audit and in information systems management it should be only a small step to the provision of environmental information. The areas that should concern us are: the production of management information for environmental reporting; valuation mechanisms for environmental investment; the disclosure of the environmental policies and the setting of the policy framework; the provision of environmental audits and the auditing of environmental accounts. This can be accomplished by the expansion of existing syllabi to ensure that the elements of ethics and environment appear contextualised in each relevant area. This has advantages in that it gives an underpinning knowledge and philosophy that pervades the entire education and training experienced by the student. That approach, in isolation, does not ensure that sufficient emphasis is given to the problems and opportunities presented, leaving much of the learning to chance and the vagaries of the examination structure and content. There is no evidence, by way of a module / paper title, that due emphasis has been given to the topic within the structure of the qualification. A higher level paper that draws together all of the disparate elements from all the earlier papers enabling the student to consolidate and make relevant accumulated knowledge is necessary. This will both benefit the student in terms of academic and professional development, and also give credence to the qualification by demonstrating a focus and commitment to the issues. However that small step may require a large change to existing paradigms and approaches to training but is necessary to the effective promotion of the profession, both as a caring and thinking profession, and as one that is professionally rounded and competent to address issues concerning future reporting and disclosure requirements.

Notes

(1)   Jones M., "Going green in the USA", *Certified Accountant*, November 1993, pp.33-34.

(2)   B&Q Environmental review, *How Green is My Front Door*, November 1995.

(3)   Rothby B., "Environmental Auditing, another lost opportunity?", *Certified Accountant*, November 1995.

(4)   Campanale M., "Cost or Opportunity", *Certified Accountant*, November 1991, pp.32-33.

(5)   Owen D., Gray R., and Adams R., "Corporate environmental disclosure", *Certified Accountant*, March 1996, pp.18-22.

(6)   Thorn EMI "Focus on the Environment '95", London. 1995

(7)   Winpenny J.T., *Values for the Environment - A Guide to Economic Appraisal*, HMSO, London, 1991.

(8)   Rice A., "The beached buoy", *Times Higher*, 31 May 1996.

(9)   Davies J., "Exclusive: shock headlines induce horror", *Times Higher*, 31 May 1996.

(10)   Biswas A.K., and Agarwala S.B.C., *EIA for Developing Countries*, Butterworth Heinemann, Oxford 1994.

7 Environmental Education: Where Does it Fit in Decision-Making?

Deborah A Blackman
Principal Lecturer in Human Resources, Southampton Business School

Tara G Fleming
Lecturer in Business Ethics, Southampton Business School

It is the intention of this chapter to explore several key areas: why business decisions should now reflect environmental issues which impact upon organisational sustainable success; the increasing, and unyet fully realised, potential importance of education in future managerial decision-making; and how indeed this can be incorporated into the curricula of the next millennium.

The issue of environmental damage is now considered to be of fundamental importance to global governments and commerce alike. In 1988 Senator Albert Gore[1] said "*The fact that we face an ecological crisis without any precedent in historic times is no longer a matter of any dispute worthy of recognition*". It has long been the case that the Earth's natural resources are used to further humankind's development and achievement; and this is extremely apparent with the creation of organisations to meet the needs of the ever-demanding consumer. It is not the purpose of this chapter to apportion blame to the present environmental catastrophe that looms before us; suffice to say that the Earth evolved to sustain life - the most intelligent of which is that of humans; however, until recently humans have, albeit unwittingly, been obliterating the ecological system which created them. The Brundtland report in 1987[2] argues that acidification in Europe may now be so advanced that it is irreversible. A quarter of the Earth's rainforests have been destroyed in the last thirty years[3]. Estimates indicate that global temperatures will increase by between 1.5 and 4.5 degrees centigrade by the middle of the next century, caused by the increased release of gases by human activity[3]. Also ozone depletion is increasing the number of reported skin cancers; and scientists estimate that the ozone layer over Europe has thinned by 18%. One could also add to the list the incidences of large-scale disasters which have caused untold damage such as the nuclear explosion at the plant in Chernobyl in 1986; Union Carbide's plant poisonous gas leak in Bhopal in 1984; and the Sea Empress oil spill off the southwest coast of Wales in 1996.

However, mankind is not doomed. We have it within our powers to halt the process; and the last three decades hold testimony to this with country collaboration over future development. In 1972 the United Nations conference entitled Economic Development and Environment, held in Stockholm, led to the formation of the United Nations Environment Programme (UNEP), and categorised the fear of post-war economic growth and its effect on the Earth's survival. The formation of the Ecology Party, later to become the Green Party, was a response to ecological scientists, who calculated that survival of the planet could only be achieved through zero-growth[4]. At the time this idea received little credence as it was felt to be politically and economically naive[3]. A more palatable alternative to the increasing crisis has come in the form of 'sustainable development'. This concept was first named in 1980 in the International Union for the Conservation of Nature's (1980) World Conservation Strategy. This particular phrase has been so widely used, and become so all-encompassing, that it threatens to mean nothing at all. However, within the business context sustainable development means "*income generation while maintaining the (natural and man-made) capital base*"[5]. The United Nations' Brundtland Report, from the World Commission on Environment and Development (WCED) (1987) has become a milestone in the marrying of the concepts of economic development and environmental strategies:

> "*It is impossible to separate economic issues from environmental issues; many forms of development erode the environmental resources upon which they must be based, and environmental degradation can undermine economic development*"[6]

The 1990s have seen the formulation of policies and determined action to meet the needs of the environment and the economy. The June 1992 Earth Summit held in Rio de Janeiro, otherwise known as the United Nations' Conference on Environment and Development (UNCED) brought together the largest number of government and state leaders ever assembled, to discuss and agree action on sustainable development. The awareness that governments must be at the forefront of environmental management was not disputed; however, the onus is also upon the business community:

> "*Business will play a vital role in the future health of this planet. As business leaders, we are committed to sustainable development, to meeting the needs of the present without compromising the welfare of future generations*"[7]

It is one thing to make these claims, but it is another to have the ability and knowledge base with which to carry out action. The cultural norm of business practice is not, as yet, fully conducive to environmental management, as the managers who make the decisions often do not have the information to make the action environmentally correct. What essentially is being explored here is the relationship between the decision and its surroundings - the ecology of decision-making. The importance of education is to enable future employers and employees within organisations to think through the impact of a decision in order to be able to maintain a balance within the environment and achieve a viable return.

How this can be achieved is open to question within organisational literature. Hoffman[8] states that corporations must not isolate themselves, but business must develop and demonstrate moral leadership. Earlier in this book Zhu[9] promotes the need to expand the scope of all decision making in order to reflect wider issues including environmental ones. Bowie emphasises a belief that consumers must take a key role in changing what they buy, and this will, in turn, influence managerial environmental decision-making[10]. Conversely, Porter and van der Linde[11] promote the concept of 'Resource Productivity' where managers stop merely paying lip service to the idea of environmental concern when making managerial decisions, but treat it as a core issue. Their argument is that where sustainable development is seen as a necessary evil people are not innovative enough in their solutions; but where managers are seeking 'closed loop' solutions, many of these benefit both the organisation and the environment. The message is clear: responsible environmental management does not follow from simply rules and regulations; it involves a clear attitude and cultural change by organisational decision-makers. This change needs to come from the recruitment of graduates who have an increased and enlightened environmental awareness which places, now, the onus on education to supply the environmental managers of the future. The concept of a need for 'industrial ecology' is further discussed by those promoting the Earth Day initiatives[12].

The need for enhanced environmental education is further highlighted by the findings of Badaracco and Webb where surveys on recent graduates elicited the fact that

> *'the young managers resolved the dilemmas they faced largely on the basis of personal reflection and individual values, not through reliance on corporate credos, company loyalty, the exhortations of senior executives, philosophical principles, or religious reflection'*[13]

It seems apparent, therefore, that decisions are not as a result of in-house organisational learning, but of graduates already having their own agenda. This is achieved through 16 years of education and socialisation. If environmental education is fully adopted into the curricula then this knowledge is carried to the organisational setting and therefore such issues will automatically be considered when decisions are being taken. It is important to first outline how decision-making takes place, to highlight the importance of education prior to organisational entry in achieving sustainable environmental strategies.

For many years the concept of decision optimisation in order to promote the ability to make 'rational' decisions has been proposed. Although criticised heavily[14; 15; 16], decision theory continues unabated, with managers attempting to reduce the unpredictable variables in order to reach an optimum decision. Any decision can be affected by certain predictable variables (see Figure 1).

Figure 1

Time	------------------|	Accuracy and
Process	------------------|_____	Appropriateness
Knowledge	------------------|	Of Decisions

It is necessary to explore each of these variables in order to comprehend fully the inability to understand and control the decision-making process within organisations, and why decision-takers have to rely on previously obtained information.

Time

The issue of the time involved when making a decision is one that offers many dilemmas for the practitioner, but there is the possibility, within reason, of controlling this particular variable. The major way in which the time frame affects the decision taker are to do with the time allocation they have in which to take the decision. The shorter the time frame the more irrational the decision is likely to be as there is little time to think around the issue[17]. There is also the time pressure associated with what other activities the person has to do in any given period. This can be handled to some extent through the development of time management; however in an increasingly competitive environment where often many decisions need to be taken within the same time frame it is difficult to prioritise. The less freedom there is to cogitate in a peaceful environment the less likely it is that new information and ideas will be sought to frame the decision. This time pressure is forcing the individual towards a 'satisficed' decision based upon what they already know[18]. If this information base is limited then an organisation cannot be sure that the decision taker has made the best, most rational decision necessary.

Process

Many organisations have put together formal decision-making processes, such as formal codes of practice, to reduce the problem of ambiguity over what decision takers are supposed to do. However, these procedures often have little effect as people are not always aware of the process they should be following, and also because the people involved are ambiguous and unpredictable in what they read as to the correct course of action. In the case of the former, more training and manuals may be put into place to try and communicate what is the correct modus operandi; but this can usually take place after it has become apparent that the system has broken down. In relation to the latter concern, it can be seen that the same process will have very different solutions. If this is applied to an operations management model:

INPUT -------- PROCESS -------- OUTPUT

it can be seen that individuals are in fact the input, and as every input is different, it therefore follows that different outputs are inevitable.

A practical example of this can be seen when people decide on a travel route in the car. They will all have the same atlas and usually an identical road map. However, there will be lots of ways that people will choose to go. Most of the differences will come from the entry behaviour displayed by the drivers when they commence the route. If they have never been there before they may choose the simplest route, or they may not like travelling on motorways, so choose a more indirect route; they may get instructions from someone else, but choose to deviate from this in order to visit certain places; or they may decide to stay on a route they have already used before for as long as possible even if it means the journey will take longer. The output here is fixed - the final destination; but if the process is flawed then the travellers may not even end up there. The idea that the process is open to an infinite number of interpretations, of which only a few have been mentioned here, means that there is a reduced potential for control. In an organisational setting the inability to control this process means that one can never assume the best decision has been made. This can have a profound effect upon organisational effectiveness and efficiency, including from an environmental viewpoint.

Knowledge

People are expected to make rational decisions on the basis of predetermined information and values. The overarching assumption is that information and values are a constant. The reality is that a truly rational decision can never be reached for anyone other than that of the individual decision taker. What is perfectly rational for one is ludicrous to someone else. This is often due to the notion of limited rationality[16]. The idea that not everything can be known, and that decision-making is based on incomplete information about alternatives and their consequences, is not new. Managers attempt to solve this problem by the gathering of more information to present the full picture, and thereby reduce the uncertainty that a wrong decision will be made. According to Feldman and March, in their study of organisational information gathering for decision-making, organisations are inherently limited for 6 reasons:

1. Much of the information that is gathered and communicated by individuals and organisations has little decision relevance.

2. Much of the information that is used to justify a decision is collected and interpreted after the decision has been made, or substantially made.

3. Much of the information gathered in response to requests for information is not considered in the making of decisions for which it was requested.

4. Regardless of the information available at the time a decision is first considered, more information is requested.

5. Complaints that an organisation does not have enough information to make a decision occur while available information is ignored.

6. The relevance of information provided in the decision-making process to the decision being made is less conspicuous than is the insistence on information. In short, most organisations and individuals often collect more information than they use or can reasonably expect to use in the making of decisions. At the same time, they appear to be constantly needing or requesting more information, or complaining about inadequacies in information[19].

The second problem concerned with knowledge or information is the idea of conflict of interest. An organisation is a coalition of individuals and groups pursuing different objectives[16, 20]. Those with knowledge try to shape decisions to meet their own ends, and sustain their own power base[21, 22]. The political arena in which decisions take place; and the availability and use of information, imply that the only constant within rational decision-making is the notion that a rational decision will never be made.

What can be concluded is that the knowledge acquired through the organisational setting is often only useful to further individual political ends and does nothing to enhance organisational effectiveness, and in fact serves to hinder. In an environmental context it seems that little is achieved if left in the hands of present day managers with present day mind sets. This is particularly relevant within a wider agenda of postmodern individualism which has emerged from the 1980s. The concern with the 'self' is now more prevalent than ever, and educating a nation on the collective responsibility of the environment is increasingly difficult. Within a time framework that impedes greater awareness, and a process which seems indefinable, the only way to provide sustainable development is through education at an earlier level.

Education of the young is fundamental here as they are still malleable and very open to new ideas. It is a pity that one can lose this ideal time to educate as, as one ages, receptiveness reduces. There is a pool of young, aware talent that can be educated both to be managers and to make the right ecological decisions for the future.

Certain concepts have emerged recently which have tried to explain the importance of education to future environmental survival. 'Environmental Literacy' and 'Ecological Literacy' are words used to describe the education of a nation in environmental concerns.

"Not only are we failing to teach the basics about the earth and how it works, but we are in fact teaching a large amount of stuff that is simply wrong"[23].

It is hoped that future educational policy will reflect the need for a more environmentally aware society. It is argued that an environmentally literate citizen *"will have a blend of ecological sensitivity, moral maturity and informed awareness of natural processes that would make her or him unlikely to contribute to further degradation of natural processes at either individual or corporate levels"*[24]. The education that is received in schools, colleges and universities is in order to prepare young people for what they might need and experience within society. It is vital that students are made fully aware of the environmental concerns as this is likely to have an enormous impact on their future activities.

It is important to note that environmental education is not something lacking from the curricula, however, at present it is failing on two counts. Firstly, educators have tended to view the environment as *"a set of problems which are: (1) solvable (unlike dilemmas, which are not) by (2) the analytic tools and methods of reductionist science which (3) create value-neutral technological remedies that will not create even worse side effects"*[25]. It is hoped from this analysis that the results will be desirable to all parties concerned. This is not necessarily the fault of the educators, as they are also conforming to the ideal of rationality and compartmentalisation of information. The problem is that the student becomes convinced that all problems are solvable; and that responses need only be reactive as opposed to proactive[26]. This is not possible where the environment is concerned, as was demonstrated earlier. The graduates produced within this form of education will continue to make the same mistakes, as they are still environmentally illiterate.

This issue is further compounded by the second problem with present environmental education. Often it is seen as an add-on, an extra. This is particularly prevalent within secondary and higher education which is discipline-based. This is not the issue at primary school level where disciplines are interlinked to provide children with a broader picture. However, this is abandoned at secondary school level, and further removed at undergraduate level. Throughout the education process students are taught to become more focused on specific areas. At primary school there is the need to encourage the development of an awareness of a wide variety of disciplines; at secondary school one is then required to make choices about which areas one would further like to explore, and certain subjects are dropped. At the university level one often becomes focused upon just one area. It is thought that the intake of knowledge is best confined to a few disciplines in order to prepare for the specificity of working life. To concentrate on one or two disciplines allows a fuller depth of analysis which increases one's knowledge base and therefore allows greater accuracy in decision-making.

Whilst at primary school a child may learn about the environment within a wider disciplinary setting, this may then be lost within disciplines such as history, politics, economics and so forth, which traditionally have not associated themselves with environmental concerns. Where it is possible to study the environment as a discipline within its own right there is a tendency to recruit those students who are already, to a certain extent, environmentally literate. This only produces a certain number of people who have environmental knowledge within their mind set, and therefore only a few decision makers with the right information to hand.

In order to make environmental literacy a reality, there must be an education system where students are aware of the inter-disciplinary nature of their learning. No subject should be taken on its own as a single entity, some specialist disciplines are already broadening the context of study and this trend would need to be widened for engineering, accountancy etc. In this way a study of the environment and of environmental responsibility can then be included within many disciplines[27] in order that by the time students become managers of any type of organisation, and via any subject route, they have a full knowledge of the consequences of their actions upon the environment whether they be working in economics, accounting, human resource management, law or marketing. In this way the manager will understand that the environmental crisis is not a problem that can be solved, but one which can be halted.

The need for this holistic approach is recognised by educators themselves as being the most effective way forward to improve management decisions[28] "*Environmental issues are regarded rightfully as interdisciplinary*" is also outlined by CERI[29] and Pizzlatto and Bevill when they studied the teaching of Business Ethics: "*if students are faced with ethical issues through multiple courses then they exposed to diverse ethical dilemmas: and only then will students be equipped to transfer this learning to their lives after college*"[30].

"*In fact, the role of the university in defining what knowledge consists of in modern societies is so central that environmental education is seriously impeded until the universities regard environmental science as a serious topic*"[31].

How Could This Improve Decision-Making?

With this awareness of what could happen with an improved, inter-disciplinary approach in all forms of education we can revisit the model in Figure 1 and see how value can be added to the decision-making process for the industrial ecology. The common goals to enhance the efficacy of all the elements of the decision (and achievable via education) seem to be to increase the availability of the information[32] and to develop a high feeling of 'valence' in the mind sets of all managers[33].

Time

Availability of information will allow managers to make faster decisions but they will in fact be better ones. The reasons for this are two-fold: firstly, the need to take a decision will not be frightening or worrying as the level of certainty as to what is right will be much clearer to employees who have had wide ranging and broad based experience. Secondly, instinct as well as reason is likely to give the appropriate decision as practice via cases will lead to an already considered opinion. High valence will also increase decision making speed because anything thought to be important will be addressed faster and in preference to other issues[34].

Process

Practice in taking environmental decisions within safe, educational environments will lead to enhanced awareness and will enable future managers to determine the best route for a specific required output (for example, the optimum passage plan in a car). Rather than deciding, almost randomly, from imperfect knowledge, more informed plans can be made. Another advantage is that where a strategy has been identified as desirable by an organisation (e.g. an environmental policy) it is more likely to be implemented in a coherent way throughout the organisation.

Knowledge

A multi-disciplinary education system allows an increased knowledge base and develops a coherent mind map within young managers who do not need to gather further information in order to make a decision; but have an inherent sense of what is right in terms of the environment. This avoids the limitations that some authors have felt organisations exhibit. Also students have been educated to avoid the political arena of management decisions, or at least not to make political decisions at the expense of the environment.

Oppenheimer[35] stresses the need to develop connectedness: linking areas of knowledge with each other to allow managers to recognise the importance of issues. This can be an on-going subject for management development which will underpin high valence levels within employees over time. Informed decisions will enhance the organisations' chances of sustainable success as the benefit for the majority can be pursued.

As indicated earlier, Bowie suggests that consumers should drive environmental policies within organisations. Currently people are as ill-informed as consumers as they are as managers or employees. Increasing the knowledge-base via the educational process addresses both of these issues: managers will take environmental decision-making seriously and consumers will be in a position to demand that organisations make environmentally sound decisions. As Porter and Van der Linde have suggested no longer will companies merely pay lip service to environmental concerns, as both managers and consumers will be enforcing sustainable development from both within and without the organisation.

Conclusion

In order to achieve sustainable success organisations are increasingly asking for multi-disciplinary managers as they continue to delayer, and empower their workforce to make more decisions within a more ambiguous, nebulous framework. The environmentally literate educational system proposed is one that is vital to organisational success, enabling as it will more coherent and informed decision-making at all levels of the organisation.

Sustainable development is not a current management fad but is, in fact, a survival mechanism for the planet. Successful companies in the next millennium will be those that integrate environmental considerations into all aspects of management and development[36].

It is, in reality, achievable but it does demand that the educators are educated, and this will involve investment from government and industry. It will also involve academics in breaking down barriers of disciplinary rivalry and developing a commitment to collaboration. As yet there is much to be done with regards to research which combines environmental management with traditional subjects. With the increasing competition for academic output it is hoped that academic researchers will utilise an under explored, but vital area.

Notes

(1)   Gore A. (1989) "What is Wrong With Us?" Time January 2, p66

(2)   Brundtland G. (1987) *Our Common Future*, OU Press, Oxford

(3)   Beaumont et al. (1993) *Managing the Environment* Butterworth-Heinemann, Oxford

(4)   Meadows et al (1972) *The Limits to Growth*, Univerrse Books, New York

(5)   Beaumont et al (1993) *Ibid*, 19

(6)   Brundtland G. (1987) *Ibid*, p 30

(7)   Business Council for Sustainable Development (1992); p xi

(8)   Hoffman W.M. (1991) "Business and Environmental Ethics" *Business Ethics Quarterly* Vol 1, Issue 2, 169-184

(9)   Zhu Z. (1997) "What should we bring to environmental eduction?" in *Environmental Education and Training*, Ashgate Publishing.

(10)   Beauchamp T.L. & Bowie N.E. (1993) "*Ethical Theory & Business*" (4th ed)

(11) Porter MIE. & van der Linde C. (1995) "Green and competitive, ending the stalemate." *Harvard Business Review* September-October, pp120-134

(12) Editorial- The Earth Day Series (1995) "Industrial Ecology" *Environment.* December 1995, Vol 87, No 10, pp16-19.

(13) Badaracco J.L. Jr. & Webb A.P. (1995) "Business Ethics: A view from the trenches" *California Management Review,* Vol 37 No.2 Winter, p9

(14) Trueblood R.M. & Cyert R.M. (1957) *Sampling Techniques in Accounting,* Englewood Cliffs, Prentice Hall

(15) Morgenstern O. (1963) *On the accuracy of economic observations,* 2nd ed, Princeton, Princeton UP

(16) March J.G. (1987) "Ambiguity and Accounting: The Elusive Link between Information and Decision-Making" *Accounting, Organisations and Society,* Vol 12, pp153-175

(17) Keerstholt J.H. (1995) "Decision making in a dynamic situation: The effect of false alarms and time pressure", *Journal of Behavioural Decision Making,* Vol 8, pp181 -200

(18) Robbins S. (1996) *Organizational Behaviour,* Prentice-Hall, 7th edition, pp150-151

(19) Feldman & March (1981) "Information in Organisations as Signal and Symbol", *Administrative Science Quarterly,* Vol 26, p177

(20) Cyert R.M. & March J.G. (1983) "*Behavioural Theory of the Firm*", New York, Prentice Hall

(21) Akerlof, G. (1970) "The market for 'lemons': qualitative uncertainty and the market mechanism" *Quarterly Journal of Economics,* 89, pp488-500

(22) Rothschild, M (1973) " Models of market organisation with imperfect information: a *survey" Journal of Political Economy,* 81, pp1283-308

(23) Orr (1992) *Ecological Literacy; Education and the Transition to a Post Modern World,* State University of New York, p85

(24) Brennan A. (1994) p5 "Environmental Literacy and Educational Ideal" *Environmental Values* Vol 3 p5

(25) Orr, *ibid,* p89

(26) Blackman D. & Fleming T. (1995) "Business Ethics: Necessary Evil or Business Tool?" in Armistead C. & Teare R Eds Services Management: *New Trends and Perspective* Cassell

(27) DFE (1993) Environmental Responsibility - an agenda for FE & HE, *HMSO,* pp 6-10

(28) DES (1981) Environmental Educations - a review *HMSO,* p34

Environmental Education: Where does it Fit in Decision-Making?

(29) C.E.R.I. (1995) Environmental Learning for the 21st century, *OECD*, p89

(30) Pizzolatto A. B. & Bevill S (1996) "Business Ethics: A Classroom Priority?" *Journal of Business Ethics* Vol 15, pp153-158

(31) C.E.R.I. (1995) *Environmental Learning for the 21st Century, OECD*, p89

(32) Sutherland S. (1992) *Irrationality, the enemy within.* Constable, pp15-33

(33) Vroom V.H. (1964) *Work and Motivation*, New York, John Wiley

(34) Finegan J. (1994) "The Impact of Personal Values on Judgments of Ethical Behaviour in the Workplace" *Journal of Business Ethics* Vol 13, pp747-755

(35) Oppenheimer M (1995) "Context, Connection and Opportunity in Environmental Problem Solving", *Environment*, p10-38

(36) ECOTEC (1996) Environmental Management Services for Corporates

8 The Impact of Teaching Ethics and Environmental Accounting

Lynda C Helps
Senior Lecturer in Accounting and Finance, Manchester Metropolitan University

The Changing Role of the Accountant

The role of the accountant has changed dramatically over the last 20 years. It is not enough to be merely a technical expert in accounting matters, as more emphasis is being placed on the advisory capacity of the individual. Accountants, as well as identifying with the profession, developing knowledge, skills and values of the profession, must possess communication skills, intellectual skills, and interpersonal skills. The professional accountant must understand the environment in which he/she works and recognise the ethics involved to be able to make value based judgements. Accountants must help communicate the reality of companies environmental problems and assess possible financial consequences on the business. The role of the accountant is now part of an interdisciplinary team, concerned with ethics, the environment, and the wider society as a whole.

The accountancy profession has expanded in recent years and assumes an even larger role in the conduct of social and economic affairs. The profession serves the needs of the community by producing accounts for shareholders, the government and other users. Accountancy is the interpretation of events,and accountants must possess communication skills to include both the receiving and transmitting of information and concepts. Nowadays, accountancy professionals need to understand the complex interdependence between the profession and society, so that they can interact with diverse groups of people. This will lead to improved understanding of social forces affecting society and the profession. "The behaviour of a profession towards its environment is a matter of perception of that environment. Once an image of that environment has been established, then behaviour will be determined by that image and frame of reference that it creates".[1]

The Environmental Protection Act 1990 has increased the personal responsibilities of every person who has control of waste at any stage of production to disposal. Failure to take all reasonable steps to prevent the illegal disposal of certain types of waste and not to observe this duty of care,is a criminal offence. The accountant may have to explain the potential costs and benefits of a company's environmental policies to the general public, who have become increasingly concerned over environmental issues. Communicating environmental effects in financial terms, including liabilities, is necessary, as more and more ethically screened investment funds are developing in the UK. More investors now consider a companies' environmental performance as equally important as a company's profitability record. Hence sound, reliable financial data is needed on current environmental issues. This ensures investors do not turn attention away from "our" company, and that protestors do not turn their attention onto "our" company.

Because of increased public concern over environmental issues, the accountant, in my opinion, has an ethical duty to communicate the financial consequences of a company's environmental policies. Hence ethics and environmental accounting issues are closely linked, and it is important that accountants are aware of their responsibilities in these areas. The accountancy profession has a responsibility to develop guidelines for its members, in the public interest, on standards of environmental accountability and ethics, and newly qualified accountants should be aware of:

1. Personal and social values and the process of inquiry and judgement.
2. Ethical and professional responsibilities.
3. Policy, social and environmental issues.
4. Technical requirements, such as standards set by the Accounting Standards Board (ASB).

The Institutes have already introduced elements of environmental accounting and ethics into their examination structure, and the following considers the development and impact of teaching ethics and environmental accounting the on education of accountants.

The Development of Environmental Accounting and Ethics Education

The major challenge for the development of accounting education in the 1990s, is the introduction of the teaching of ethics and environmental accounting. The two concepts could be linked in that it could be argued that if significant environmental risks were not disclosed, then the accountant is being unethical. The accountancy Institutes have clear guidelines on ethics, but there is less regulation on environmental matters. Environmental issues are clearly related to the financial aspects of the company, and therefore the accountant will have to ensure effective disclosure of environmental issues. Environmental accounting policies must be properly implemented, as misstatements resulting from environmental issues may damage the company's standing in the community, and bring into question the fact of business ethics. It is clear that environmental pressure groups have an impact on the business community. "Management should establish clear lines of responsibility on environmental matters and give a board member overall responsibility for such issues [2]. Details of environmental performance with resultant revenue or capital expenditure may now be disclosed in published accounts, to show the company's commitment to the environment.

Environmental and social accounting goes "beyond" the mere maximising of profits. Many companies are now keen to show their "green"credentials and do so via their annual report. They believe by doing so they can gain support of the public, shareholders, and employees, and so gain an advantage over their competitors. Some companies do provide details of environmental policies, although as yet, the ASB has not issued any standards on environmental accounting policies. Employees are concerned to work in non-hazardous environments, whilst investors are becoming more unwilling to invest in companies, who they perceive as harming the environment. Environmental reporting covers one area of social reporting, and companies are increasingly disclosing the environmental impact of their activities. Market sources may require the provision of such information in future, following the increase in ethical investment.

Companies are thus responding to social concerns regarding their activities. Students must be able to recognise issues in accounting that have ethical implications, and should develop a sense of moral obligation and responsibility in their professional work. Moral issues related to business, including environmental matters, must be exposed to accountancy trainees, as if they are not aware of the many ethical dilemmas they will face, they are likely to make a bad or poorer decision. Students need to think about ethical issues, and how they, as individuals will face these issues, before they are confronted with real world dilemmas. James Rest (1986) "advocates that one goal of an accountancy course is to advance the moral development of students studying in the profession"[3].

Many people feel that ethics is an in-built quality that cannot be taught. However, some would argue that studies should link the moral perception and judgement with real life behaviour. It is essential that students should consider current controversial issues, such as environmental accounting, which are relevant in the accountancy profession. Accountancy students are provided with reasoning skills, which they can employ to make better reasoned decisions, when confronted with moral choices. The accountancy Institutes publish codes of ethics which students are expected to comply with, and hence they are aware of their duties towards society, and thus have a better understanding of their professional duties. However, in an enlightened society, we must recognise that laws do not necessarily prescribe ethical behaviour, or reflect the ethical norms of society. As a society "we would like to think that the gap between legal and ethical norms is small, but a number of situations in recent years involving insider trading, foreign corrupt practices and hazardous waste disposals, suggest that legal behaviour is sometimes subject to a lesser standard, than what is considered to be ethical behaviour"[4].

In the past there were many aspects of the profession which were learnt through experience, by an "on the job" approach. Many would argue the case for introducing aspects of ethics and environmental accountability at an earlier stage in career development. Ethical theory could and is being introduced at the training stage, so that students are exposed to ethics prior to becoming members of the Institutes. Video case studies, relating to ethical issues are already being used by the Institutes. Mary Armstrong (1993) suggests that "ethics can be taught on existing accountancy course, as either an integrated aspect of the course, or as a separate course"[5]. At the moment ethics and environmental accounting are included as part of the Institutes syllabuses. They are not currently separate subjects, but are covered as integrated subjects, as shown in the following summary.

The Institute of Chartered Accountants England and Wales - ICAEW

The ICAEW clearly believes that ethics and environmental accounting are important aspects of their exam structure, as they have introduced these topics into their examination structure. The ICAEWs Environment Research Group has produced a discussion paper on the subject of reporting environmental matters, which reflects their commitment towards this topic. The report entitled Business, Accountancy and the Environment (1992), considers the ICAEW's policy and research agenda into the subject of environmental accountability. "Given the variety of information likely to be needed by the various stakeholders with an interest in a company's environmental policy and performance, and the different media for communicating this information, we take as a central theme in this report the issue of how far the established reporting cycle to shareholders is an appropriate vehicle for communicating information about environmental matters. We also seek to identify the potential contribution of the accounting and auditing profession in developing corporate reporting to include such information"[2].

The ICAEW's foundation aspects of education include the following papers:

1. Foundation Accounting and Auditing considers professional and ethical aspects, in connection with the independence of the auditor.

2. Introduction to Business provides students with an understanding of the economic, legislative and informational environment surrounding business. The syllabus considers the economic and business environment, including the inter-relationship of functional areas in business.

The intermediate examination papers include:

1. Accounting and Information Systems which includes a guide to professional ethics, with regard to integrity, objectivity, independence, confidentiality, and changes in professional appointments.

2. Financial Planning and Control considers performance measures, including financial and non financial, and how these are communicated to interested parties.

Final examinations include the following aspects of environmental accounting and ethics, as part of the exam structure:

1. Auditing and Financial Reporting looks at legal and professional considerations, including the students ability to advise on the duties, rights, responsibilities and liabilities of the auditor. The student should be able to discuss current issues in auditing, accounting and financial reporting (including ethical issues and environmental accountability), as identified by the professional bodies and professional press. Students must take into account the "guide" to professional ethics, expectations of professional conduct, and the commercial and business environment.

2. Business Planning and Evaluation ensures students can identify the internal and external factors (including multiple objectives) which currently, or in the future may impact upon an organisation's performance. All significant costs and benefits of environmental protection programmes are considered. Students must also consider how environmental factors could affect an overseas investment decision.

On the broader international front, the environment continues to be a major controversial topic, as seen at The Earth Summit in Brazil in 1992. Governments continue to be concerned about environmental policy, and this impact on business activities is becoming more apparent. As companies become increasingly concerned with environmental policy, it is desirable that reporting should include details of practices, achievements, with quantifiable environmental targets and performances wherever possible. Perhaps this will only arise if there is regulatory control through accounting standards.

R Gray's ACCA research report (Greening of Accountancy 1990) signified the first response of the accountancy profession for research into the implications of the growing environmental issues. The ACCA, along with other UK Institutes, is concerned with codes of ethics and the impact of environmental accounting on the accountancy profession.

The Chartered Association of Certified Accountants - ACCA

The ACCA's examination structure shows its concern with ethics and environmental accounting in the following papers:

1. Paper 4 - Organisational Framework considers the types of organisations and their environment, and the way in which the environment impacts on business activity.

2. Paper 6 - Audit Framework looks at professional codes of ethics and behaviour, at an introductory level.

3. Paper 9 - Information for Control and Decision Making considers the impact of the environment on the accounting information system.

4. Paper 12 - Information and Strategy includes the effect of an international environment on organisations. The effect of the external environment on corporate strategies and plans is also reviewed.

5. Paper 13 - Financial Reporting and Environment considers ethical issues which students are likely to encounter within the accountancy profession.

The Chartered Institute of Management Accountants - CIMA

Some companies produce separate environment brochures, as well as disclosing information in their annual reports. Such information is not required to be disclosed by company law, accounting standards or the Stock Exchange, so it is up to company management whether or not they disclose environmental policy. Companies are increasingly addressing environmental issues and including some quantitative information. CIMA recognises that if disclosure of environmental policy is to become normal practice, then this must be addressed in their examination structure. CIMA also considers the question of ethics, both from a student and business point of view.

1. Paper 3 - Economic Environment looks at market and financial environments, including the international environment.

2. Paper 4 - Business Environment and Information Technology - The emphasis of questions will be how consumer and pressure group activity may affect and possibly constrain business activities. A business's relations with its consumers are important in the modern day environment.

3. Paper 9 - Financial Reporting includes environmental accounting issues and the implication of these for the management accountant.

4. Paper 11 - looks at the organisations strategy, on the basis of the environment in which the organisation operates. Organisations must determine which aspects of the environment are relevant to them.

5. Paper 13 - Strategic Financial Management analyses the changing, competitive, business environment necessary to formulate financial strategy.

6. Paper 14 - Strategic Management Accountancy and Marketing tests the student's ability to relate the organisation to its environment. The candidate's appreciation of the environment, the forces that influence it and how this impinges on the organisation is likely to be tested. This paper considers social responsibility and professional ethics within the accountancy profession.

The government has a major part to play in legislative matters (including fiscal incentives), and in regulating a wide range of environmental issues, and it has an important influence on reporting environmental performance. The importance of public accountability and disclosure requirements under the Environmental Protection Act 1990 means that waste management activities have to be licensed with local waste disposal authorities. This act increased the personal responsibility of directors for the disposal of waste, and increased public concern over environmental issues. It could be argued that the accountant has an ethical duty to communicate the financial consequences of a companies' environmental policy. Hence it is important that accounting students experience aspects of ethics and environmental accountability, as part of their training programmes. Accountancy students, training with all the UK Institutes, must understand the relevant ethical issues and mechanisms for enforcing ethical standards in environmental accounting. CIPFA recognises the increased public concern over environmental issues, and includes the following as part of its examination structure;

Chartered Institute of Public Finance and Accountancy - CIPFA

The foundation syllabus includes the impact of ethics and environmental accountability in the following subjects:

1. Financial Accounting considers the nature and environment of accounting, by looking at the current role of accounting in society and business. Ethics and independence are also considered.

2. Management Accounting includes the nature and environment of management accounting including the use of non-financial information.

3. Business Environment aims to develop an understanding of the economic and legal environments in which a business operates. The paper includes an introduction to the national and international environment influences on business activity.

Professional levels develop the themes of ethics and environmental accountability further in the following papers:

1. Auditing considers social and environmental audits. The auditors' responsibilities already extend to consideration of environmental factors as auditors are required to draw attention to any uncertainties, in their audit report.

2. Business Strategy develops an understanding of the environmental and financial framework in which the student operates. The competitive environment is considered together with the needs and desires of the customer.

3. Treasury and Tax Management includes accountability and ethics, under portfolio management, together with long term financing problems.

Conclusion

The Institutes must continually review their examination syllabuses to ensure all students have an awareness of environmental and ethical issues. Qualified accountants must also be encouraged to promote good environmental management reporting and auditing. In future companies' environmental performances will come under more scrutiny because of public pressure groups. There are advantages in providing environmental information as part of the annual report, but a company must ensure information is reliable, consistent and comparable. The impact of teaching ethics and environmental accountability is ongoing for the student and qualified accountant alike, so that an environmental culture is developed throughout the accounting profession. The overriding objective in developing course content should be to create a base upon which continued learning can be built. Hence it is important that examination structures continue to reflect the problems which will face the accountancy student in respect of environmental accounting and ethics involved.

Notes

(1)   Burchell et al. _Accounting in its Social Context_ 1985.

(2)   Professor Richard Macve and Anthony Carey. _Business Accountancy and the Environment! A Policy and Research Agenda,_ ICAEW 1992.

(3)   James Rest _Moral Advances in Research Theory,_ New York 1986.

The Impact of Teaching Ethics and Environmental Accounting

(4)   H Langenderfer and J Rockness Issues in Accounting Education, Vol 1994, no 1 USA, Spring.

(5)   Mary Armstrong. Journal of Accounting Education, USA Spring 1993.

(6)   ICAEW, CIMA, ACCA and CIPFA examination structures 1995.

9 Why and How Organisations Provide Employees with Environmental Education

Tara G Fleming
Lecturer in Business Ethics, Southampton Business School

Deborah A Blackman
Principal Lecturer in Human Resources Management, Southampton Business School

Introduction

This chapter is concerned with the environmental education awareness raising of employees within an organisation during their working lives. Chapter six was directed at the issue of environmental education for the development of undergraduates who will become tomorrow's managers. The authors aim to explore a continuation of this theme by addressing two key issues: firstly, there is the problem that "environmental education has not yet been sufficiently incorporated into the elementary, secondary, and general university curriculum to develop an environmentally knowledgable and concerned citizenry"[1]; and secondly, "even when such widespread environmental education does occur, it will not be entirely sufficient to prepare individuals to deal with environmental issues as managers"[2]. Corporations have a vital role to play in the successful utilisation of environmental management through the education of their workforce, and this chapter will outline some of the ways that this can be achieved.

Why Educate Employees?

The first question to address is why environmental education is necessary for employees and organisations at all. The previous chapters in this book have addressed this issue in some depth. Increasing awareness through scientific study has shown the consequences of an industrial age which discovered the economic benefits of the exploitation of this planet's natural resources and survival mechanisms. What has emerged is an understanding that if something is not done to try halt the process of the earth's mutilation there will no longer be an earth to exploit. The implications for an organisation are manifold: the law now expects compliance with an increasingly complicated and growing legal framework; stakeholder perspectives of the importance of sustainable development and more responsible profit-making have led to shareholders, customers and employees being more likely to expect an organisation to be 'environmentally correct' or choosing to take their custom or labour elsewhere. Furthermore the old adage that 'all publicity is good publicity' is not something that Union Carbide, after the gas leak in Bhopal[3], would probably agree with.

Currently, although the pressures upon organisations to be more environmentally responsible are self-evident, the current response of companies is varied and lacks continuity and consistency. The approach is often accused of being piecemeal, and of having a lack of holism within one organisation let alone across industries. Solutions are described as "applying Band-aids to immediate problems (cleaner emissions, waste reduction) rather than joining in the attack on root causes (global poverty and grossly uneven levels of development)"[4]. Problems are treated with stop-gaps or placebos rather than as a real strategy to help prevent reoccurrence of the 'graze' or 'cut'. Such responses are necessarily reactionary and short-term - often applied to a small part of the organisation. The realisation that some wounds do not heal regardless of how many times they are bandaged is not one that many companies or the individuals who work within them have registered. How many employees actually know where the goods they are selling come from? How many would actually care if they did know? The key issue is that people are not aware of the big picture because they are unaffected by it and it fails to have any significant impact upon their lives. It has been suggested that where a "green organisational culture"[5] does exist it tends to flow unevenly and in different directions[6,7] not only within the company itself, but the departments also. Strategic management of green issues is also fraught with anomalies, in that the decision to go green in order to maximise competitive advantage is rarely considered as a dominant philosophy - "it usually has to be haggled for by a 'committed', but ever vulnerable champion"[8]. According to Shrivastava, the only green certainty is legislation, which demands that environmental issues are recognised as relevant to the organisational agenda [9], however corporate obedience to the law does not necessarily imply refraining from efforts to weaken the nature of newly proposed laws and regulations[10]. The rather pessimistic view is that the paradigm shift in organisational thinking and practice has yet to come[11], and that the ardent rhetoric declaring the doomed outcome of the planet has been largely unshared by managers, in as much as short-term managerial profit-making schemes are understood. What has been argued is the understanding that this situation will change on the basis of new green managers appearing within organisations, in what is termed as a shift in organisational ecology[12] whereby there is inevitable organisational change through selection and replacement. Therefore the future looks promising for business behaviour in an environmental context; nevertheless, there is a time gap whilst these managers fully grasp the communication of environmental values - and this is time that some would argue this planet can ill afford. The process must begin now, through the education of the existing workforce - not merely waiting for the 'new environmentalists' to arrive.

If a company is, therefore, to promote safe, socially aware and proactive environmental policies then they must start from the basis that an organisation is a human construction, and that all actions that companies take are the consequence of human understanding and motivation[13]. The employees of an organisation must comprehend what has to be done, why it has to be done and what that means for them.

General findings which have emerged from research on energy conservation, which could also be applied to other environmental behaviours[14], have found that monetary rebates and incentives appear to be highly effective means of encouraging energy conservation. Reliance on education, persuasive communication, and moral appeal alone has generally been insufficient in promoting widespread conservation[15]. Taking an example of smoking, it can be illustrated how convincing this research is. Many intelligent and well-educated people know that smoking is harmful not only to the smoker, but the people who come in contact with the smoker. Despite education, whereby children are shown graphic pictures of diseased lungs and people dying of cancer, persuasive communication used in the form of advertising and parental and peer pressure, and moral appeal through the campaigns of anti-smokers etc, people continue to smoke. The incentive to smoke is greater than that to give up. The reality is that it is difficult to comprehend that which one cannot see, and easy to deny risks when one remains unaffected by the consequences. Only when faced with an alternative incentive can an individual make the decision to give up ie. saving the money spent on cigarettes for a holiday; watching someone close die a slow, painful death; or seeing one's own premature baby. Human motivation for action is essentially egoistic and hedonistic and deals with the short-term as this is the only point of reference that is real. As has been mentioned previously, organisations are human constructions and motivation for action has to be relevant or it will lose significance. An organisation will not choose to make a decision for the future if that means going under in the present. Instant gratification is far more rewarding than future policies which may or may not work. In order for environmental policies to be successful, organisations and their employees must see short-term goals leading to long-term aims - there must be achievable and desirable rewards at each short stage if behaviour is to change.

Another finding implies that the amount of feedback regarding the amount saved from energy conservation appears to be important as "individuals seem to be poor self-monitors of their level of consumption"[16]. There are plenty of people who keep very accurate records of their incomings and outgoings on a monthly basis. Again this relates to personal consumption. What is missing is what that consumption actually means. When so many kilowatts of electricity are used what does that mean in terms of fossil fuel burned or nuclear waste produced? It is impossible to know everything about every product that one uses, but ignorance leads to waste. If individuals could see that each time they turned a light off instead of leaving it burning, in terms of a reduction in pollution or waste, it would provide an incentive for continuing. Within organisations if employees were made more aware of the monitoring processes and could see a benefit to the company in terms of savings, again relating to monetary incentives, then environmental policies have more chance of working. Water consumption is dramatically reduced when households move on to water meters and can see their usage as a real and now manageable cost.

It does seem apparent that the acceptance of personal responsibility for energy conservation actually enhances pro-active environmental management. Schwartz argues that the immorality of harming others is only recognised when individuals are aware that their actions are harmful and accept some responsibility for these actions and their consequences[17]. Although there has been some agreement, with relation to environmental behaviour, in particular the acceptance of personal responsibility, there are criticisms over whether the norms are moral or environmental, and indeed whether environmental norms should be considered as moral norms[18]. However the implications of this research are that moral norms can only be activated when individuals can perceive that they are doing harm. If this can be extended to the environment, then the only way for individuals to curb harmful environmental behaviour is to understand exactly what it is they are doing wrong. If they have no knowledge of the consequences of their actions then they are unlikely to demonstrate positive environmental behaviour.

On the basis of this research Rands has formulated a set of implications for organisations:

"Reward systems are important in promoting pro-environmental behaviour and implementing corporate environmental policies. A variety of motivational and control approaches are required, because of the diverse nature of individual environmental motivations.Effective environmental evaluation systems are critical. Organisational structures and systems should simultaneously fix specific environmental responsibility with roles and job descriptions and promote and encourage acceptance of personal responsibility for company environmental responsibility in areas beyond one's job"[19].

Rands goes on to mention that managers must make sure that employee understanding and skills are developed within an environmental framework. However he maintains that although practised within organisations the interpretation of environmental education may be too simplistic, as merely receiving distributed factual, written information has been found to be largely irrelevant to improving or altering behaviour[20]. In many organisations this is partly due to the volume of paper being circulated around the organisation. Much communication is ignored, as to act on all of it would be to ignore one's core tasks. A similar problem is being found with electronic mail where so many messages are being sent that only ones sent by known and respected sources are read and received. Another potential reason for the communication message being ignored is that the language used and reasons given to the employees as to why this is important alienates them.

For example Government policies to improve the environment have been used by many organisations as a bench-mark for environmental managers to communicate their position through legal initiatives. The law demands that organisations look at their use of resources and waste to see where recycling can be achieved and where less harmful pollutants can be utilised or removed altogether. This punitive approach to environmental education can be extremely effective in terms of creating more environmentally-friendly companies. "But for the corporate actor, legislation is fertile ground for the exercise of managerial talents for negotiation, game playing and persuasion"[21].

The implications of this are that compliance is not understanding, and without understanding there is no hope for long-term positive measures - as punitive motivational strategies merely instill feelings of impingement. Without a greater awareness of the benefits of the legal regulation and government policies, companies will endeavour to avoid the long arm of the law, as it threatens a free market economy. Such messages may influence the organisation but the people needed to implement the changes may not feel sympathy with the issues couched in these terms.

Rands concludes that "personal acceptance of responsibility for harm caused by action may be a critical factor in encouraging pro-environmental behaviour"[22]. This argument is valid but in terms of providing a framework for achieving this within an organisational setting, aside from the recognition that this must be an holistic approach, he leaves other authors to continue. It is the authors' intention to explore research into the study of learning in order to 'bridge the gap' between legal compliance and personal responsibility, and then to demonstrate how this has been achieved by some companies.

How to Effect Behavioural Change

"Learning is a relatively permanent change in behaviour that occurs as a result of practice or experience[23]. There are two important aspects to this: the fact that learning leads to an alteration in what an individual does and that for this to happen an individual needs to have been involved in the learning process. The concept of practice, however, needs careful definition. Assumptions have been made by organisations that repetition and conditioning of behaviour will lead to compliance[24, 25] which will in turn lead to 'understanding'. In fact learning must be cognitive if it is to be applied in a meaningful way. According to Kolb and Fry[26] *"learning involves the labelling or relabelling of immediate existential experience"*. This can explain why within organisations memos do not work and why distance makes it worse. Managers find something has not changed and so send the same memo again. If no learning took place the first time it is unlikely to take place on future occasions. Repetition will not change anything if the message was not understood initially; only by changing the communication system is the learning likely to take place. Some would argue that, in fact, where a message is constantly sent but not understood it can actively lead to subversion of other learning as other messages will be taken less seriously. This can be seen where an instruction is given but then not enforced when it is misunderstood. Future orders will be ignored as the first one was not perceived as real.

If repetition will not lead to learning what will? Bateson stated that *"An explorer can never know what he is exploring until it has been explored"*[27]. The implication is therefore, that in order to fully comprehend anything experience is vital. Kolb[28] states that there are four stages of learning: experience; observation of and reflection on that experience; analysis of the key learning points arising from it; and the consequent planning and trying out of the new behaviour. This, however, presupposes that people want to learn. Gagne[29] stresses that for successful learning there must be a drive or motivation to learn. Without this the process will not be undertaken in a meaningful way.

The implication is that once the drive is in place learning will become self motivated: *"learning is a human activity which least needs manipulation by others. Most learning is not the result of instruction. It is rather the result of unhampered participation in a meaningful setting "*[30]. This definition, although widely recognised within the analysis of learning, is one that is not commonly practised. It stresses the need for self-management and individual focus in the success of learning. The permanence of learning outcomes is derived from the initial desire to learn. It is generally accepted that needs are either intrinsic: hunger, sleep etc. and are driven from within, or are extrinsic leading us to behaviour for external reasons (seeing others eating something we like makes us want to eat even if we are not hungry)[31]. Thus, the objective of development and education will be to create a desire to be environmentally aware which will act as an extrinsic need to be fulfilled when making decisions on any matter. The stronger the need the more predictable will be the behaviour patterns created. Thus an organisation that wishes to pursue proactive sustainable development needs to create a high valence within employees, to be motivated to be environmentally aware, who are the key element in achieving organisational memory[32].

The logical progression of this is if employees cannot actually see how what they are or could be doing is affecting the environment, the desire to act in the way that will most benefit the long term environment, and by implication the organisation, will diminish. Black and Synan confirm this need for ongoing confirmation of behaviour *"through concrete action it is possible gradually to build the organisational capacity of an organisation, its capacity to co-operate, to make decisions and implement them effectively. This strengthening of the organisation depends upon both understanding and the accumulation of experience in concrete action*[33]. The planning of development must therefore not only include knowledge but also practice and concrete experience. This underpins not only the view that this is what is currently missing within the organisations, but also that a development system in order to achieve understanding will still be needed in the future. Even when incoming employees have environmental awareness and understanding they will need opportunities to have this knowledge re-affirmed and to practise how their current employer wants the knowledge to be used. Recent examples of ethical companies, who were allegedly found to have made mistakes (Marks and Spencer, Body Shop and the Co-operative Bank) demonstrate how without understanding at all levels unwanted behaviour may still occur.

So far this chapter has argued that for organisations to become effective environmental managers, behaviour will have to change throughout the employee structure. Yet at present most organisational educational systems will not achieve this. The level of experience does not run deeply enough to allow cognitive learning to change behaviour and the implication is that the desire to learn is not yet fundamental to the employees' value systems the figure below shows a model for environmental education practitioners which might help to address these problems; and case examples from two companies will demonstrate possible solutions.

Environmental Strategy Implementation

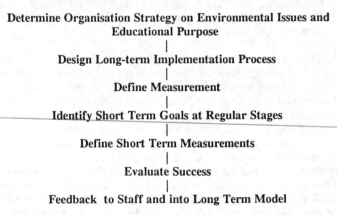

Determine Organisation Strategy on Environmental Issues and Educational Purpose

|

Design Long-term Implementation Process

|

Define Measurement

|

Identify Short Term Goals at Regular Stages

|

Define Short Term Measurements

|

Evaluate Success

|

Feedback to Staff and into Long Term Model

Determine Organisation Strategy on Environmental Issues and Educational Purpose

As with any form of training or development it is vital to determine firstly, what behaviour is desired, and secondly, why it is desired. It is easy to spend a lot of money without achieving the desired effect as demonstrated earlier by the ineffectiveness of memos. An organisation needs to be clear on how committed to the goals it really is. Some companies are actively addressing ways of enabling realistic learning to promote responsible environmental behaviour. One such is B&Q plc. which has decided that it is committed to be not only environmentally aware in everything it does but also to act as a leader for other organisations within this sector. It sees the organisation as being responsible for the future of the limited resources left in the world. Its first concrete act was to appoint Alan Knight as its Environmental Manager and then trusting him to do what was right in the long-term for the benefit of both the company and the environment.

By appointing Mr Knight there was a positive symbol to all stakeholders that the move towards sensible environmental policies was not merely a paper exercise. They could see not only was he trusted to change policies and re-invent B&Q but he was given the resources he needed as well. For example, in order to be sure that B&Q are using wood from only sustainable sources he did not just trust word of mouth but got on a plane to see for himself. Where he found forests were not sustainable he advised the suppliers on how to change if they wanted to continue having B&Q as a customer; with reassurances that what they produced in the future, by sustainable means, would be purchased by the company. This sort of initiatitive is disseminated throughout B&Q plc. in order to encourage environmental cultural change. The recruitment of a specific individual who targets environmental misdemeanours is a positive step towards B&Q's proactive stance; however, the public awareness of this behaviour creates a culture which actively encourages more people to take action. B&Q's culture provides the means by which individuals feel that it is their responsibility to be proactive.

Once the organisation has communicated what it wants to achieve then it can set up systems to develop at all levels. Boots plc. is another company that has actively chosen to educate their staff regarding the environmental issues pertaining to their products. Their given reasons include the need to provide the consumer with information; a need to promote the need for environmental care to their own staff; and the very real fact that organisational marketing benefits from environmental awareness.

The mixture of organisational egoism and altruistic motives is not unusual and does not detract from the message being sent. The overt statement of what the message is to be makes successful dissemination more probable.

Design A Long-term Implementation Process

The methods employed are fundamental to a successful environmental education programme. As was mentioned previously, the generalisation that smoking kills holds little relevance for most people; and having established that it is not only the experience that makes the generalisation real, but also the limited level of expertise reduces the desire to know and therefore decreases the need for ownership. Without the trigger there is no desire for knowledge; the design must, therefore, provide the impetus to learn as well as imparting the knowledge. The potential barriers to learning should be addressed and individual learning styles should be reflected.

Honey and Mumford outlined that a key barrier to learning may be the lack of recognition of the learning needs and styles of each individual[34]. Sometimes we try to teach by preventing something when only experience will define the real behaviour in the future for that individual. How often is a child told not to touch nettles? But only being stung will give the child the reason not to touch again. In this case the desire to experiment and gain knowledge is there but only a real experience will trigger desired behaviour.

Managers need to remember staff have different perceptions of events if they know about them at all. For B&Q plc. an example of the need to make issues real has been seen with the use of child labour in India. All brass hinges being sold in their stores were being made in a factory that was a health and safety risk and employed child labour. However, it was the only source of employment in the area. The problem can be hard for the western world to comprehend as, whilst a strategy of withdrawing at once seems initially appropriate, in fact this is too simplistic. In order to bring home the reality of the problem Mr Knight showed employees and the press pictures of the factory with the children and himself. The strategy was that these Indian village scenes depicting the situation in conjunction with a familiar person would make it at once more real and more compelling. Observers would realise why B&Q plc. could not just pull out and why they were actively helping the factory to change its ways - by investing time and money in a project which requires all children to attend school at least one afternoon a week, and improving the working conditions of the employees. For it to be real staff must then be shown where they fit in - i.e. care in choosing suppliers, explaining pricing structures to customers and educating them, boycotting other companies etc.

Boots plc. also demonstrate this awareness to reflect learner styles and the need to vary the message. Earlier in the chapter it was stated that merely sending memos may not work and they recognise this. In order to maximise the effect of staff development they send the same message in several different ways: an information pack, team briefing, development seminars and new product introductions. Other methods seen in companies are staff newspapers, focus groups, enabling first hand experience of issues via participative and action-based learning, pictures, case studies and seminars. Everything is aimed at giving experience and meaning to the situation - partly to act as a prevention tool for future disasters. Diamond, a manager for Union Carbide, commented *"We will learn more as we gain actual experience"* following the Bhopal disaster[35]. How much better if we can learn via simulation and preclude the need for the disaster itself.

True cognitive learning is time consuming and so a realistic assessment of the time frame involved needs to be made. Companies will probably be more willing to have a more complex approach if they accept the view that this type of development will be on-going and not a short-term message. Companies that are achieving substantial change have accepted this long term view and are creating acceptance into the core values and competences of the company.

Define Measurement

It will be hard to define the desired outcome but it is a key part of success. Mr Knight of B&Q plc. stated that for them the success is that for each environmental issue they find they address it head on and do something about it. They then define what must be done at each level: a current issue is the selling of Peat for use in gardens. The approach is two-fold; firstly reducing sales of peat, which is easy to measure; secondly, through the communication of their staff to educate the consumer to not only accept the organisational decision, but to positively welcome it. This entails educating staff to understand why the issue is important. Measurement is from supervisors monitoring responses and success is to always hear not only "We do not sell peat" but also "because...". Without the latter part of the response, it is obvious that employees have not engaged in cognitive learning, but are making merely conditioned responses which will not have any long-term advantages; and also customer acceptance and education will not be achieved. The desired output here is to move away from single loop learning towards double loop learning which then identifies a new questioning and informed culture[36].

Identify Short Term Goals at Regular Stages

As Rands indicated earlier for any behavioural change, whether it is the organisation or the individual there is a need for realistic, incremental incentives where interested parties can see the benefits accruing in a meaningful way. For some smokers putting aside the money they used to spend on cigarettes now to be spent on luxury items helps them to see a real benefit from giving up. It is so much more tangible than a possibility of living longer. To pick up the Indian village example more pictures and discussion every six months will show how the factory has changed, that the workers are older and that their organisation is achieving something worthwhile. It should also enable the organisation to see the extent of press coverage and it will continue to support the initiatives as well.

If targets are not broken down in some way there is a danger of a stage of implementation being missed out and staff failing to see the importance of what is happening. Once the extrinsic need is not being seen to be achieved, other needs will take precedence or an alternative behaviour will be sought to satisfy it. In either case desired behaviour may not ensue. Setting short term goals allows them to be measured more effectively.

Define Short Term Measurements

Following from defining short term goals is the definition of achievement. This allows people to feel they are being successful. If the smoker sets a target of the amount needed to go on holiday or buy new clothes this is then real. If the saving is on-going but other than the money there is no output the incentive it provides may begin to lapse.

Evaluate Success

As with all training results must be measured to ensure the model is working and learning is taking place, and that the learning is of the desired nature. One measurement may be to see how self-sustaining the development now is. For example, the organisation may encourage regular local press releases highlighting what a particular part of an organisation or set of people have been doing (for example at store level for both B&Q plc. and Boots plc.) i.e. - cleaning up the local area. They can be costed as advertorial each time cover is given and thus not only can success be measured as raising the profile but also as an amount of money that would have had to be spent if the organisation wanted to buy the space. This enables realistic feedback to be given to staff as to their achievements and to the organisation regarding the level of acceptability the ideas have.

Feedback to Staff and into Long Term Model

All models need a feedback loop in order to confirm the activities taking place and to restructure the plan as required. Each time a goal is reached or a stage completed all stakeholders need to be informed. This structure can only allow reflection and act as a theoretical base for learning to build upon. B&Q plc., as well as raising knowledge levels on specific issues, are also promoting general awareness regarding what environmental issues affect their staff and the world they live in; this is of necessity in an on-going process. The company acts as a facilitator explaining what the new issues are, enabling employees to learn more, encouraging and supporting their involvement in related movements; but never forcing integration with the local communities, environmental groups, the teaching of issues or involvement at all. B&Q argue that only voluntary involvement and compliance will create lasting environmental policy, as Illich was quoted earlier as saying, manipulative learning is ineffective in the long-term.

What they wish to do is to build a questioning culture which will benefit both the employee and the business. The more interest individuals have in environmental issues the more they will support organisational aims to improve themselves. For those looking to achieve successful environmental auditing and to achieve the quality thresholds this will be an important move forward. The focus is not only upon individual learning but on organisational learning too. Employees need to feel they have a responsibility for the environment and that they are empowered to do something. There must be ownership which can only be achieved via a cognitive awareness of what is being done. Awareness of an individual's role and seeing what they can actively achieve towards the whole is fundamental to change. There is much discussion by companies currently of sharing the goal or 'mission'. For this to be achieved effectively there must be an understanding of what the person contributes to the big picture of the organisation's achievements and a clear delineation of what the real goals are. This is an ongoing process and must be added to the general feedback.

Conclusion

Organisations cannot afford to ignore the increasing need to incorporate environmental awareness into their decision making at all levels. The impetus to act comes from both within and without the organisation as the impact of our short term business decisions upon our long term planetary future becomes clearer. Instinctive actions from informed employees will be the way to facilitate such behaviour and this can be gained via cognitive learning. How to achieve this via education then becomes the question.

In many ways the argument being put forward is to follow the basic principles proposed by Rands: the formulation of reward systems; the variety in motivational and control methods; the use of effective environmental evaluation systems; and an organisational commitment to the encouragement of personal responsibility for environmental concerns: but to add the element of experiential learning in a meaningful way. Even when there is far more awareness and acceptance of the importance of environmental education leading to the recruitment of educated employees, without regular up-dating and re-inforcement, the message may be lost or not applied as a company may wish. The need for a proactive, on-going approach to organisational education is clear and the opportunity to manage the organisational memory banks should not be ignored. The model cited, whilst simple, stresses the need for a long-term approach that is realistically staged to promote motivation and understanding. Performance can be defined as motivation multiplied by ability: regular up-dating should maintain motivation and therefore performance.

This book is exploring the issues of Environmental Education and whether it matters. This chapter shows that for the future of everyone it not only matters that organisations educate their staff but that it is vital that they do so as an on-going, long-term project.

Notes

1. Rands G.P. (1990) 'Environmental Attitudes, Behaviours, and Decision Making: Implications for Management Education and Devlopment' in *The Corporation, Ethics and the Environment* edited by Hoffman W.M., Frederick R. & Petry Jr. E.S., Quorum Books, p270

2. ibid, p270

3. Diamond S. (1985) 'The Bhopal Disaster: how it happened' *New York Times*, 28 January, pp 1,6,7

4. Davidson D.K. (1990) `Straws in the Wind: the Nature of Corporate Commitment to Environmental Issues' in *The Corporation, Ethnics and the Environment* edited by Hoffman W.M., Frederick R. & Petry Jr. E.S., Quorum Books, p65

5. Shrivasta P. (1994) `Castrated Environment: Greening Organisational Studies' *Organisational Studies* Vol 15, No. 5, p724

6. Aldrich H.E. (1992) `Incommensable paradigms? Vital Signs from Three Perspectives.' In *Rethinking Organisatoins* edited by Reed M. and Hughes M, Sage.

7. Martin J. & Siehl C. (1983) `Organisational Culture and Counter-Culture' *Organisational Dynamics* No 12, pp25-64

8. Shrivasta op cit, p724

9. ibid

10. Bowie N. (1990) `Morality, Money and Motor Cars' in *The Corporation, Ethnics and the Environment* edited by Hoffman W.M., Frederick R. & Petry Jr. E.S., Quorum Books

11. Khu, (1970)

12. Hannam M. & Freeman J. (1989) *Organisational Ecology*, HUP

13. Ritzer L., Kammeyer J. & Yetman P. (1982) `*Sociology, Experiencing a Changing Society*, Allyn & Bacon

14. Shippee G. (1980) 'Energy Consumption and Conservation Psychology: A Review and Conceptual Analysis', *Environmental Management*, 4, pp 297-314

15. Stern P.C. & Aronson E. (1984) *Energy Use: The Human Dimension,* Freeman

16. Rands op cit p274

17. Schwartz S. H. (1970) 'Moral Decision Making and Behaviour' in *Altruism and Helping Behaviour: Social Psychological Studies of Some Antecedants and Consequences* edited by Macauley J. & Berkowitz, New York Academic Press

18. Buttell F. H. (1987) 'New Directions in Environmental Sociology', *Annual Review of Sociology* 13, pp 465-488

19. Rands op cit, p 275

20. March J.G (1987) `Ambiguity and Accounting: The Elusive Link Between Information and Decision Making' *Accounting, Organisation and Society*, Vol 12, pp153-175

21. Shrivasta op cit, p 724

22. Rands op cit, p 283

23. Bass B.M. & Vaughn J.A. (1967) *Training in industry; the management of learning* Tavistock Publication

24. Pavlov I.P. (1902) 'The work of the digestive glands' cited in Robbins S. (1993) *Organisational Behaviour*, Prentice Hall

25.   Skinner B.F. (1971) 'Contingencies of Reinforcement' cited in Robbins S. (1993) *Organisational Behaviour*, Prentice Hall

26.   Kolb D. & Fry R. (1975) 'Towards an Applied Theory of Experiential Learrning' in *Theories of group processes* edited by Cooper C., Wiley & Sons p34

27.   Bateson G. (1972) *Steps to an Ecology of Mind*, Ballantine, p xvi

28.   Kolb, op cit

29.   Gagne R.M. (1965) *Conditions of Learrning* Holt, Rhinehat & Winston

30.   Illich (1973), p 39

31.   Schemerhorn et al. (1994) *Managing Organisational Behaviour*, Wiley & Sons, pp167-193

32.   Walsh J.P. (1991) 'Organizational Memory' *Acadamy of Management Review*, Vol 16, No 1, pp57-61

33.   Black D.H. & Synan C.D. (1996) 'The changing practices of organisational development' *Management Accounting*, May Vol 74 pp34-5

34.   Honey P. & Mumford A. (1986) *The manual of learning styles* 2nd ed, Peter Honey

35.   Diamond, op cit, p7

36.   Argyris C. & Schon D. (1981) *Organizational Learning* Addison Wesley

10 Learning to Choose a "Greener" Route for Small Organisations

Jason Palmer
Eclipse Research Consultants, Cambridge & Department of Manufacturing & Engineering Systems, Brunel University

Rita van der Vorst
Department of Manufacturing & Engineering Systems, Brunel University

Introduction

A single person can make a big difference to an organisation's environmental impact; anyone can leave lights or heating on unnecessarily, anyone can pour chemicals down the drain. So all employees need to learn how their organisation has an impact on the environment, and how their own work decisions can amplify or attenuate this impact. Learning is therefore a key part of changing behaviour towards the environment and a valuable first step for organisations to include all employees in an environmental initiative. The standards for environmental management systems - BS 7750[1] and the Eco-Management and Audit Scheme (EMAS)[2] - both explicitly recognise the need for training, but the employees of small organisations often fail to perceive the importance of learning opportunities and training[3].

Small and Medium-sized Enterprises (SMEs) have been lifted onto the political stage in recent years for a number of reasons. The Employment Department defines a *Small* Enterprise as one that employs less than 200 people - making up more than 99% of UK companies and 55% of employment[4]. The small business sector prospered and grew markedly during the 1980s; more than 1 million additional small companies were created between 1979 and 1989[5]. It is thought that these new firms were responsible for generating much of the growth witnessed over this period.

Michael Gilbert[6] and others have suggested that SMEs are more flexible and thus better able to adapt to the demands of a changing economy; SMEs account for some 38% of non-farm Gross Domestic Product generated by the private sector[7]. It is reasonable to assume that these organisations are responsible for a significant proportion of the environmental impact of UK industry.

However, there is some concern that smaller companies may be at a disadvantage when it comes to improving their environmental performance. Certainly, their attempts to change trail far behind those of larger organisations. The destination and routes towards best practice for SMEs may differ from the options open to big business, but the incentives for action are similar. Better environmental practices can reduce costs, increase sales, cut the risk of prosecution for malpractice[8], boost employee morale and improve an organisation's image. Some large companies are putting their (smaller) suppliers under increasing pressure to 'green' - especially the large companies intent on EMAS or BS 7750 certification. To respond to these incentives, and to capitalise on the benefits of environmental action, SMEs need to train. But small organisations face difficulties that would be unlikely to affect larger counterparts. Specifically:

1. there is often intense pressure on resources; both time and money, to the extent that neither are available for investments in training,

2. there is rarely an individual appointed with particular responsibility for either training or the environment,

3. management and staff do not recognise 'what's in it for them' if they succeed in changing.

Commentators note that SMEs that train their employees are in the minority[9] [10]. There is a variety of different obstacles to training of all kinds in smaller companies. Given the importance of training to improving environmental performance, the real question for training providers is how to motivate small organisations into action; how to entice them into an environmental learning opportunity.

Pursuit of Environmental Information

Training is one part of an organisation's constant search for information. While the pursuit of information cannot be taken as a direct proxy for training needs, it does provide an indication of where an organisation sees it has a gap to fill. A survey by the British Chambers of Commerce [11] investigated the extent to which SMEs can access and exploit environmental information sources. It found that three quarters of companies employing less than 50 - i.e. 'small SMEs' - consider themselves to be well or adequately informed about environmental issues and how their business is affected. This high figure has undoubtedly been biased by the high proportion (more than 70%) of companies of this size that are involved in operations not normally associated with high environmental impacts: retailing, service provision, farming, etc. Perhaps it is unrealistic to expect many companies of this type to embark on sophisticated training voyages towards the distant and unfamiliar shores of environmental management - unless they are compelled to do so by legislation.

However, in spite of this high proportion of small companies who claim to be adequately informed or better, it emerged during the survey that 43% of respondents have sought information, guidance or advice on environmental issues. Most of this group required information on legislation (78%). 68% also required advice on health and safety issues. This is clear evidence that small organisations do recognise a need for information and thus by implication, learning opportunities - at least about environmental legislation and health and safety. Indeed, those who have taken concrete action in pursuit of information may represent just a small proportion of the total numbers who have recognised their requirement for information; there may be many others who are unable to search out information because they lack either time or knowledge about where to look.

If small companies recognise the need for information, why don't they create learning opportunities to help address this shortfall?

Obstacles to Training in SMEs

There are numerous problems facing SMEs that are less pronounced - or even non-existent - in larger counterparts. Many of these represent real barriers to generating learning opportunities generally, environment-oriented learning in particular.

1. Most small organisations have very limited time and funds available to invest in training and other costly learning mechanisms.

2. Decision-makers in smaller companies are more reluctant to make investments. Often this is because the capital they have put into the business is at stake. This means that the need to satisfy both owner/managers and employees is even more important than usual.

3. Most SMEs have not delegated responsibility for environmental good practice - or indeed training - to a particular individual.

4. And they will probably be unfamiliar with non-technical training that is not task-oriented; training that is essential for their employees to fulfil their role - control a machine, assemble a component, use a piece of software, &c.

In addition, there are several less tangible obstacles to learning in small organisations resulting from their perception of training. The Further Education Unit[12] felt that they are reluctant to train because of fear about how employees will react - either that they will expect more money, or that untrained employees will complain about unfair treatment. The FEU also said that SMEs do not have the expertise to recognise when training is required.

Small organisations often do not perceive that their activities have a significant impact on the environment. Moreover, since the environment tends to be peripheral to core activities, it is easy for them to neglect it - to relegate environmental issues down the agenda in favour of other concerns.

It is claimed that 30% of small companies fail to meet all environmental legislation[13]. In some cases, this could be used as a lever to motivate SMEs into action. However they may fear 'coming clean' about their environmental (mal)practice, and will be wary of approaching a training centre associated with regulators in any way. The incentive to act for the sake of compliance alone is unlikely to generate top management commitment to environmental training.

Avoiding the Obstacles - Orienting Learning to Meet SME Needs

Are there real benefits for 'greener' SMEs; to individuals and especially to owners and managers? Can training - as part of a basket of learning opportunities - show individuals in an organisation what they should do and how to do it? How can we steer around the obstacles and tempt the would-be green SME with our route for environmental training?

Benefits in 'Greener' SMEs

The central advantage for individuals in any organisation that comes from environmental initiatives is an improved public image. This increases personal pride: both in day-to-day work and in the corporate identity. General staff job satisfaction and motivation often increases, which can translate into rising levels of productivity and even fewer sick days being taken. Managers too feel better about their work and, if they are closely associated with the organisation in the local area, a concern for the enviroment may add polish to their reputation in the community.

Owner/managers also stand to gain financially from 'greening' in four ways. First, from the direct cost savings that result from more efficient use of energy and materials. Second from the reduction in risk - of prosecution, expensive clean up, or compensation payments - that can follow an environmental accident. Third, from the market place advantages that sometimes come with an improved public image. And fourth, from greater employee commitment to the organisation and possible ouput hikes that may result.

The Training Package

Perhaps the most difficult part of keeping the ship from the rocks is ensuring that a learning opportunity wins the approval necessary for sustained use. This can only happen if it is successful in arousing employee interest in environmental training. This is, in fact, a two-fold objective. First, it should convince the user that training represents a profitable investment of time. Second, it should persuade that environmental training is as valuable - or more valuable - than training in other subjects.

Where training is available, individual employees will prefer topics where they see clear benefits for themselves. Preferences are likely to be for training which will:

1.   appeal to current job aspirations, including increasing levels of responsibility,
2.   make the job easier, faster, or more interesting, and
3.   improve on-the-job safety.

This means that in order for a training package to be successful, it should be presented in a way that relates to these preferences. There should be explicit links between learning outcomes and these three criteria. And linking information to key functions and responsibilities is likely to attract a warmer reception for training.

A more problematic individual motivator is the opportunity to improve employees' transferable skills and thus their employment prospects. This runs counter to management priorities and could reinforce fears of losing staff after training - especially in flat hierarchy SMEs with few opportunities for promotion. This point therefore needs to be dealt with sensitively;

emphasising to decision makers the potential for motivating the workforce and attracting high calibre employees in the first place.

If the audience is unfamiliar with training that is not directly related to tasks - like the organisational guidance that is often needed to improve environmental management[14] - it may be necessary to dovetail technical and non-technical issues in a single course.

Course material should emphasise the way your audience's operations do impact on the environment, that their activities can fall foul of environmental law. And it should explain how failure to 'green' their operations risks blackening their name in the eyes of key stakeholders. This will help to overcome the perception that the environment is not an issue for small organisations.

In order to win over a SME's confidence, it is best to dissociate training providers from regulators; playing down links with Local Authorities or the Department of the Environment. Providing opportunities for participants in training sessions to speak frankly about success and failures will also be invaluable here - participants will see that they are not alone in confronting similar issues.

Giving employees the ability to identify savings for themselves is said to be critical to the success of initiatives aimed at clean and profitable production in industry[15]. Thus training should address precisely this issue - it should equip SME representatives with the skills to identify benefits that are ripe for them, in their own particular circumstances. Tailoring courses to particular sectors of industry will probably be useful in this instance: by including only the environmental impacts - and the scope for improvements - that apply to individual sectors.

Presenting the Training

Equally challenging is the task of getting a training package into the SME - by persuading decision makers that the benefits will outweigh the costs. Given the small organisation's problems in raising investment capital, setting an acceptable price is of immense importance. Similarly, the training must make minimal demands on employee time - perhaps in half-day slots over a number of weeks. If possible, delivery should be flexible enough to align training with low workload periods. A likely scenario for small company training would be where a single motivated employee attends a training course, to train others on their return to the company. Course providers can support this kind of cascade model, either by offering 'train the trainer' type packages, or by assisting learners when they become in-house company tutors.

The training's marketing is critical to calming the seas around SMEs. Publicity material must underline the potential for real financial benefits from adopting a more conscientious stance towards the environment. The FEU think that training should be seen as a product. Thus, like a product, it is necessary to sell the benefits; decision makers will buy what a product will do for them, not what a product is (FEU, 1991: p.21). The learning outcomes must emphasise opportunities to improve profitability that will follow directly from the competences the package will pass on. Similarly, course material and cases studies for (finance-oriented) decision makers must relate to a model of environmental performance improvements that tie in to the bottom-line. For training aimed at those with operational responsibility, the money bias may be less important, but the benefits to individuals must be underscored with equal weight.

Any contact with a potential audience for training - whether face-to-face or written communications - should be used as an opportunity to motivate and inform. If the audience lacks expertise to recognise a training need, then guidance of this type should be provided. If they fear an employee backlash from training initiatives, then they should be reassured about the consequences of training in the field, relating this to similar organisations with a history of training.

Emphasise SME Advantages

Potential learners in SMEs may seek to delay setting sail for as long as possible - because they assume that only bigger boats can navigate the threatening waters of environmental management. This means that efforts to persuade both decision makers and other employees of the value of environmental learning should also stress the advantages SMEs have over their larger peers:

1. breadth of responsibilities and greater cohesion
2. fewer people to convince - less 'social inertia'
3. their adaptability - less 'mechanical inertia' too.

In small enterprises, employees typically have a broad range of different responsibilities, covering functions that are usually split up into different departments in larger organisations. This gives SMEs a head start in setting up an integrated approach to change. It also means that co-ordinating different functions - all of whom play a role in environmental initiatives - is far simpler.

The obvious advantage for the small company embarking on a journey of environmental improvement - or, indeed, any change programme - is that there are fewer people around to convince that change is required. This means that communicating the change is more straightforward. Where training is necessary it can be delivered more quickly and more cheaply than is the case for a larger firm.

The greater simplicity of operations and less mechanical hardware used in small organisations present real advantages when it comes to any change initiative. It is probably easier to spot opportunities for improvements, and it is also easier to effect the changes required. Admittedly, financing investment may be problematic, but there are often no cost or low-cost measures from which organisations can reap great rewards in terms of environmental improvement.

Conclusions

Smaller organisations face increasing pressure to improve their environmental performance. Customers, banks, insurers, local residents, legislators, and especially corporate purchasers are calling for change. They are already developing a preference for recognised 'green' companies. Training, within a basket of other opportunities for learning, is one key to unlocking employee involvement and better environmental practice.

We can see that smaller organisations often lack enthusiasm for training. Yet steps can be taken to lower, or even remove, the barriers blocking entry for training in an SME. Critically, a learning opportunity has to raise awareness about broad issues that are not directly related to tasks without losing sight of business activities. Important as it is to convince managers of the value of training - before you are through the door - it is also necessary to sell the idea of training to individuals lower down the corporate hierarchy; to motivate them once you are in. So a learning opportunity must sell the benefits to individuals and show how they outweigh costs.

Training a SME to be green is difficult - arguably more difficult than training a larger counterpart. However, a firm hand on the tiller can steer around the obstacles and promote environmental good practice. And a well chosen route - including ports of call where there are opportunities for learning - should help even the most hesitant SME traveller to change direction; to a new route towards greener shores.

Notes

1.   British Standards Institution, BS 7750:Specification for Environmental Management Systems, BSI, London, 1994.

2.   The European Commission, "Eco-Management and Audit Scheme Regulations, 1836/93",Official Journal of the EC, Ref. No. 4186, 10 July 1993, HMSO, London.

3.   Confederation of British Industry, Management Training for Small Businesses, CBI, London, 1986.

4.   The Employment Department, "National Survey of Employment" (end 1989), Employment Department Gazette (1992), Employment Department, London, 1992.

5.   Beavis S., "Bleak Outlook in Middle of Road", The Guardian, (3.5.94), The Guardian Observer, London, 1994.

6.   Gilbert, M., Achieving Environmental Management Standards: A step-by-step guide to meeting BS 7750, Inst. of Management/Pitman Publishing, London, 1993.

7.   Hillary, R., Small Firms and the Environment, The Groundwork Foundation, Birmingham, 1995.

8.   Palmer, J., Green Law and Smaller Organisations:A sledgehammer to crack a nut or shooting into the wind? Eclipse Research Consultants working paper, ERC, Cambridge, 1995.

9. Department of Trade and Industry, SME Research Programme: Management training for growth firms, DTI internal paper, DTI, London, 1994.

10. Stanworth, J., Gray, C., Bolton 20 Years On: The small firm in the 1990s, Small Business Research Trust, London, 1991.

11. British Chambers of Commerce, Small Firms Survey: Environment, BCC, London, 1990.

12. Further Education Unit/Pickup, Training for Small and Medium Companies, FEU, London, 1991, pp. 18-19.

13. Smith, M., "Stimulating environmental action within SMEs", in Advances in Environmental Auditing Conference Proceedings, London, 1995.

14. Johnston N, Stokes A (1995) Waste minimisation and cleaner technology: An assessment of motivation, CEST, London.

15. Gee, D., Clean Production: From industrial dinosaur to eco-efficiency, Manufacturing Science Finance, London. 1994, p. 38.

Index

Abandonment costs 76
Academic analysis 21
Academic environmental law/lawyers 20, 21
Accountants 8, 9
    changing role 93-4
    ethical duty 94
Accounting. *See* Environmental accounting
Accounting Standards Board (ASB) 76, 94
Administrative functions 21
Advisory Committee on Business and the Environment (ACBE) 5
Agricultural chemical input 29
Agricultural Training Board (ATB) 5
Agriculture 27-38
Amerasinghe, Cecil 42
Animal manures 27, 28, 30
Animal waste disposal 27
Anthropocentricists 20
Aquifers
    nitrate movement in 34
    recharge schemes 33
Argumentation 72
Armstrong, Mary 95
"Assessment of Ground Water Quality in England and Wales" 34
Association of Chartered and Certified Accountants (ACCA) Promotion of Environmental Reporting 76
Auditing/auditors. *See* Environmental auditing/auditors
Audubon Society (USA) 6

Badaracco, J.L. Jr. 84
Bateson, G. 105
Behavioural change 105-7
Benchmarks 104
Bevill, S. 88
Bhopal disaster 108
Biological control systems 31
Black, D.H. 106
Blue Baby Syndrome 34
BNFL 16
Body Shop 106

Boots plc. 107, 108, 110
Bowie, N.E. 83, 89
B&Q plc. 75, 80, 107-10
Brent Spar 74, 78
British Agrochemicals Association 36
Brundtland report 82, 83
BS5750 80
BS7750 75, 80, 114
Burnett-Hall, R. 16
Business, Accountancy and the Environment (report) 95
Business environment 98, 99
Business planning and evaluation 96
Business strategy 99

Cairncross, F. 6
Canadian Institute of Chartered Accountants 75
Cancers 16
Cattle 16
CEB 48-9, 53
Central Environmental Authority (CEA) 43, 48
Centres of environmental excellence 13
Chartered Association of Certified Accountants (ACCA) 97
Chartered Institute of Management Accountants (CIMA) 97-8
Chartered Institute of Public Finance and Accountancy (CIPFA) 98-9
Chemical emissions 79
China, population policy 69
Chlorine 79
Civil law 22
Civil liability 25
Civil proceedings 22
Climate Change Group 14
CNEC 45-7
Coastal Conservation Act 1981 42
Codes of practice 33
Cognitive-instrumental rationality 71
Colombo-Katunayake Expressway project 53
Communication 13
Communicative rationality 71, 72
Compliance 104

Conflict of interest 86
Consumer culture 23
Co-operative Bank 106
Corporate Report 74, 80
Cost benefit analysis 35-6, 75, 77
Cost considerations 75
Criminal law 22, 25
Cropping methods 31

Dearing, Sir Ron 5
Decision-making 82-92
    improving 88-90
    knowledge in 86, 89
    on environmental issues 72
    processes 85, 89
    time in 84-5, 89
Decision-making environment and procedures 70
Decision theory 84
Degree courses 13, 14
Department of Agriculture for Northern Ireland 35
Department of the Environment 31, 32, 34, 36
Developing countries, EIA process in 52-7
Diamond, S. 108
Domestic legislation 22
Double loop learning 109
Drinking water
    House of Lords Committee Report on 36
    nitrate concentration in 32, 34
    pesticides in 36
Due diligence 37
Duty of care 76

Earth Day initiatives 84
Earth Summit (Rio de Janeiro 1992) 83, 96
Ecological Literacy 87
Ecology Party 82
Eco-Management and Audit Scheme (EMAS) 114
Economic environment 97
Employees, environmental education for 101-13
ENDS report 33
Energy conservation 103
    personal responsibility for 103
Environment Agency 12
Environmental accountability 76, 99
Environmental accounting 63, 74, 80, 94-5
Environmental Agency 35

Environmental auditing/auditors 8, 9, 63, 74, 75, 80, 81, 96, 99
Environmental behaviour 102-4
Environmental challenges 17, 25
Environmental damage 76, 82
Environmental disciplines 25
Environmental education 9, 65-73
    and environmental law education 18-19
    for employees 101-13
    programme design 107-8
Environmental expenditure and savings 77
Environmental Foundation Limited (EFL) 46-7, 49-51
Environmental impact assessment (EIA) 78, 79
    government attitude in implementation 55
    in developing countries 52-7
    information and training 56-7
    legal process 52-5
    Sri Lanka 42-4
    Upper Kotmale Hydro-Project (UKHP) 49-52
Environmental information 81, 115-16
Environmental law
    and environmental problems 19-21
    and regulation 13
    content 21
    distinctiveness 24-5
    for non-lawyers 24-5
    MA in 15
    module 15
    subdivisions 21-2
    syllabus 23
Environmental law education
    and environmental education 18-19
    essence of 17-26
    objectives 22-3
    recipients 11-16
    role of educator 22-3
Environmental liabilities 76
Environmental Literacy 87, 88
Environmental management 103, 118
Environmental policy 21, 81, 96, 97, 104
Environmental politicians 21
Environmental problems 79
    and environmental law 19-21
Environmental Protection Act 1990 93, 98
Environmental protection organisations 6
Environmental regulatory authority 25
Environmental Reporting 74, 80, 81, 94
Environmental responsibility 88
Environmental science 14, 16, 21

123

Environmental standards 80
Environmental strategy 79-80, 83, 84, 98
  implementation 106-7
Environmental thinking 65, 70
Environmental values 23-4
Ethics
  and accounting issues 94
  companies 106-8
  education 94-5
  guidelines 94
  implications 95
  issues 95
  norms 95
  teaching 95, 99
  theory 95
  video case studies 95
European Community 21
European Council Directives
  80/68 5, 34
  80/778 35
  88/708 27, 28
  91/676 27, 29, 30
European Council Regulations
  1094/88 30
  2078/92, 2079/92 and 2080/92 30
European laws 25
European Union 28, 31
Eutrophication
  problems 35
  strategy 35
Expert-deference theorists 19

Farm waste disposal 28
Farmers
  improvement of local management through
  education 38
  pollution friendly 33
Fay, Chris 78
Feedback 103, 110
Feldman 86
Fertilisers 27, 29-31, 33, 34
Financial accounting 98
Financial education 63-4
Financial planning and control 96
Financial reporting 96, 98
Financial training, needs and implications 74-81
Ford `Pinto' 77
Foundation accounting and auditing 96
Friends of the Earth (UK) 6

Fry, R. 105
Further Education Unit/Pickup (FEU) 118

Genetic damage 16
Gilbert, Michael 114
Gore, Albert 82
Government policies 104
Graham, J.D. 78
Graham case 16
Gray, R. 97
Great Lakes Water Quality Agreement 31
Green Party 82
Greening of the curriculum 18
Greenpeace 6, 78
Gross domestic product 114
Ground water pollution 34
Groundwater protection 29

Habermas, J. 70-2
Habitat Improvement Scheme 30
Hatton Catchment Nitrate Study 33
Higher education 74
Hoffman, W.M. 83
Honey, P. 108
Hope and Reay case 16
House of Lords Committee Report on drinking
  water 36
Human motivation for action 103
Human relations 66
Hydroelectric dam project. See Upper Kotmale
  Hydro-Project (UKHP)
Hydroelectric power generation, environmental
  costs 40

IEE reports 52, 53
Imperial College 14
Incinerator plant 16
Industrial ecology 84
Industrial processes 25
Industrialist-versus-regulator perspectives 25
Information systems 81, 96
Institute of Chartered Accountants England and
  Wales (ICAEW) 95-7
Instrumental rationality/actions 71
Interdisciplinary dialogue 16
Interdisciplinary environmental issues 88
Interdisciplinary strategy 17

Interdisciplinary teaching 25
Interdisciplinary teaching curriculums 9
Interface books 16
Internal world complexity 70
International environmental obligations 22
International law 21, 25
International Standards Office (ISO) 11, 12
International Union for the Conservation of Nature 83
Inter-subjective assessment 71, 72

Japanese International Co-operation Agency (JICA) 44
Jeffery, Michael 31

Kaisen 79
Kalpage, Stanley 41
Knight, Alan 107-9
Knowledge
    and rationality 71
    in decision-making 86, 89
Kolb, D. 105
Kotmale River 45

Land management practices 27
Large-scale disasters 82
Law modules 15
Lead 35
Learning process 105, 108
    small and medium-sized enterprises (SMEs) 116-17
Legal regulation 13
Legislative needs and expectations 9
Licensing authorisations 25
Liquid manure 30
Livestock density 28
Livestock levels 27
Livestock manure 29
Livestock units 28, 29
Lough Neagh 35

MA in Environmental Law 15
Ma Ren-chu 69
McEldowney 16
Macrory, Richard 14
Mahaweli River project 41
Malaria 45

Management, stages of 79
Management accounting 99
Managerial education 63-4
Mao Tse-tong 69
March, J.G. 86
Marks and Spencer 106
Meadowland Scheme 30
Measurement and monitoring 109-10
Media orientation 20
Ministry of Agriculture Fisheries and Food (MAFF) 28, 30, 33
Monitoring and measurement 109-10
Moral issues 95
Moral norms 103
Moss, Brian 35
MSc in Natural Resource Management 15
Multidisciplinary education system 89
Multidisciplinary strategy 17
Multidisciplinary teaching 25
Multidisciplinary teams 16
Mumford, A. 108

National Curriculum 74, 79
National Environment Act (NEA) 42
National Environmental Policy Act 1969 (NEPA) 42
National Rivers Authority (NRA) 28, 29, 34
    Water Quality Series Reports 33
National Trust (UK) 6
National Wildlife Federation (USA) 6
Natural Resource Management, MSc in 15
Natural sciences 13
Natural world complexity 70
Nitrate leaching 33
Nitrate movement in aquifers 34
Nitrates 27, 34, 35
    concentration in drinking water 32, 34
Nitrogen 29, 31
Non-point source pollution strategy 31
Nuclear testing 65

Objective phenomena 70
Old management 79
Ontological complexity 71
Operations management model 85
Oppenheimer, M. 89
Organisational effectiveness and efficiency 85
Outcome definition 109

Ozone layer 82

Pacific Gas and Electronic Company 75
Paper industry 79
Parliamentary Office of Science and Technology 35
Peat sales 109
Personal responsibility for environmental concerns 103, 104, 111
Pesticide containers 33
Pesticide Forum 31
Pesticides 34, 35
    in drinking water 36
    minimisation techniques 31
    spillages 33
Phosphorus 35
    stripping techniques 33
Pizzlatto, A.B. 88
Planning permission 29
Plant breeding techniques 31
Political agenda 63
Political dimension 20
    Polluter Pays principle 76
Pollution friendly farmers 33
Porter, M.I.E. 89
Primary school 88
Proactive management 79
Professional ethics 23
Profit and Loss account 76, 77
Project approving agency (PAA) 43, 48, 54

Quality performance indicators 79
Quantitative risk assessment 35

Rands, G.P. 104, 109, 111
Rationality
    and knowledge 71
    and reality 70-2
Reactive management 79
Reality and rationality 70-2
Rechem 16
Reductionism 65
Renewable raw materials 79
Report on Freshwater Quality 5
Resource Productivity 83
Rest, James 95
Reward systems 104

Richardson, D. 31
Risk perception 38
Royal Commission on Environmental Pollution
    4-5, 12, 28, 34
Royal Society for Nature Conservation (UK) 6
Royal Society of Chemistry 16

Safety standards 35
Schwartz, S.H. 103
Scientific technology 71
Secondary education 74
Secondary school 87
Self-evidence theorists 19
Set aside regulations 30
Set aside scheme 30
Severn-Trent Water 33
Shell U.K. Limited 78
Short term goals 109
Short term measurements 109
Sierra Club (USA) 6
Single loop learning 109
Skin cancers 82
Sludge and slurry operations 29
Slurry and silage 33
Small and medium-sized enterprises (SMEs)
    114-21
    benefits in `greener' 117
    emphasising advantages 119
    environmental information 115-16
    learning process 116-17
    obstacles to training 116-19
    presenting the training 118-19
    training package 117-18
Social accounting 94
Social concerns 95
Social reporting 94
Social world complexity 71
Soil compaction 33
Soil erosion 33
SPCC v *Kelly* 37
Specialist environmental education 19
Species diversity and amenities 37
Sri Lanka 39-62
    development impacts 40-2
    economy 40
    Environmental Impact Assessment (EIA)
        process 42-4
    hydroelectric potential 40
    waterfalls 41

[see also] Upper Kotmale Hydro-Project (UKHP)

State of the Environment in the European Community 31
Statement of Provisions 76
Statistical information 38
Statutory Instrument SI 1988 number 1352 30
Strategic financial management 98
Strategic management accountancy 98
Success evaluation 110
Sulphur dioxide 79
Sun Yat-sen 66, 70
Synan, C.D. 106

Talloires Declaration 18-19
Targets 109
Technical considerations 65
Television programmes 63, 74
Thompson, J.B. 71
Thorn EMI 77
Three Gorges Project 65, 66-70
    advocates 67
    alternatives 67
    approved in principle 67
    construction commenced 68
    critical and significant issues arising from debate 68-70
    irreversibility 68
    opponents 67
    technical assistance 67
Three-world complexity 71, 72
Three-world reality 70
Time in decision-making 84-5, 89
Total Quality Management (TQM) 79
Town and Country Planning Act 1990 29
Town and Country Planning General Development (Amendment) (Number 3) Order 1991 29
Toyne Report 2, 3, 23, 24
Treasury and tax management 99
Tropical rain forests 40

Understanding Our Environment 16

Union Carbide 108
United Kingdom Environmental Law Association 11
United Nations Conference on Environment and Development (UNCED) 83
United Nations Environment Programme (UNEP) 82
United Nations Human Environment Conference, Stockholm 1972 65
Upper Kotmale Hydro-Project (UKHP) 39-62
    campaign against 46-8
    EIA process 49-52
    impacts 44-6
    lessons learned from campaign against 49-52
    potential geological damage 45
    proposed site 44
    rejection and appeal 48-9

Valuation, of environmental issues 78, 80, 81
van der Linde, C. 83, 89
Vocabulary 13

Water Management policies 37
Water pollution 27-38, 79
Water quality 27-38
Water resources, integrated planning and management 37
Water Resources Act 1991 37
Water treatment blending and replacement 33
Webb, A.P. 84
Winpenny, J.T. 78
World Bank 55
World Commission on Environment and Development (WCED) 83
World Conservation Strategy 83

Yangtze River 67
Yangtze Valley Planning Office 67, 69
Yorkshire Water case 15

Zhu, Z. 83